E R M A N
M P I R E
0
100 miles
200
A U S T R I A
H U N G A R Y
A N D
The St Gotthard
he Simplon
Milan
Verona
Venice
Mantua
radella
Piacenza
Ferrara
Parma
Modena
Genoa
Bologna
Carrara
Florence
Pisa
ROME
Naples

A caricature of Dickens by André Gill

DICKENS IN EUROPE

ESSAYS SELECTED AND INTRODUCED BY ROSALIND VALLANCE

THE FOLIO SOCIETY
LONDON 1975

PRINTED IN GREAT BRITAIN
by W & J Mackay Limited, Chatham

Contents

CONTENTS

Illustrations

TO

LESLIE C. STAPLES

Honorary Editor of

The Dickensian

1945 to 1968

DICKENS IN EUROPE

Crossing the Channel

'I have been abroad in the world from a mere child, and have lived in London and travelled by fits and starts through a great part of England, a little of Scotland, less of France with my eyes open. Heaven send that some kind wind may soon blow me to Germany.'

Thus, in July 1838, Dickens wrote to Dr H. Kuenzal, who had asked him for some personal data for inclusion in his forthcoming appraisal of the German Pickwick Papers, *one of the earliest of the hundreds of translations of Dickens into every likely and unlikely language that have flooded the world from that day to this.*

And though that kind wind never blew him very far into Germany, it certainly blew him into a great many other places in Europe. Nothing could be more evocative of the essence of his wandering, wondering disposition than that 'I have been abroad in the world from a mere child . . . with my eyes open'. Already, in Sketches by Boz, *he had given evidence of those distinctive powers of observation and memory which were to find continuously maturing expression in his letters and descriptive writings, notably in* The Uncommercial Traveller, *where, with a dreamlike disregard of mere chronology and a special delight in 'all things counter, original, spare, strange', he gives his impressions of animals, places and people, not only in his own country but in Italy, France and Switzerland.*

But The Uncommercial Traveller *can often be unpleasantly realistic, and it is not, alas, with one of his most agreeable peregrinations that this book must open, but with 'The Calais Night Mail'. Writing in 1862, Dickens looks back on the hateful sea-crossings which were the inevitable prelude to any and every visit to Europe, even those by 'l'écrivain célèbre' on his way to give a fantastically successful reading of his own works. If only, with a pile of books under both arms, as in the imagination of that French caricaturist,* *he could have stepped lightly across from London to Paris! But 'l'écrivain célèbre' was no more immune from sea-sickness than the humble twenty-five-year-old tripper of July 1837 had been when he had made that first ten-day visit to France with his wife and the artist 'Phiz', and, as he wrote to John Forster*, had travelled in a post-chaise 'to Ghent, Brussels, Antwerp, and a hundred other places that I cannot recollect now and couldn't spell if I did'.*

THE CALAIS NIGHT MAIL

It is an unsettled question with me whether I shall leave Calais something handsome in my will, or whether I shall leave it my malediction. I hate it so much, and yet I am always so very glad to see it, that I am in a state of constant indecision on this subject. When I first made acquaintance with Calais, it was as a maundering young wretch in a clammy perspiration and dripping saline particles, who was conscious of no extremities but the one great extremity, sea-sickness – who was a mere bilious torso, with a mislaid headache somewhere in its stomach – who had been put into a horrible swing in Dover Harbour, and had tumbled giddily out of it on the French coast, or the Isle of Man, or anywhere. Times have changed, and now I enter Calais self-reliant and rational. I know where it is beforehand, I keep a look out for it, I recognise its landmarks when I see any of them, I am acquainted with its ways, and I know – and I can bear – its worst behaviour.

Malignant Calais! Low-lying alligator, evading the eyesight and discouraging hope! Dodging flat streak, now on this bow, now on that, now anywhere, now everywhere, now nowhere! In vain Cape Grinez, coming frankly forth into the sea, exhorts the failing to be stout of heart and stomach: sneaking Calais, prone behind its bar, invites emetically to despair. Even when it can no longer quite conceal itself in its muddy dock, it has an evil way of falling off, has Calais, which is more hopeless than its invisibility. The pier is all but on the bowsprit, and you think you are there – roll, roar, wash! – Calais has retired miles

* Later to become his biographer.

inland, and Dover has burst out to look for it. It has a last dip and slide in its character, has Calais, to be especially commended to the infernal gods. Thrice accursed be that garrison-town, when it dives under the boat's keel, and comes up a league or two to the right, with the packet shivering and spluttering and staring about for it!

Not but what I have my animosities towards Dover. I particularly detest Dover for the self-complacency with which it goes to bed. It always goes to bed (when I am going to Calais) with a more brilliant display of lamp and candle than any other town. Mr and Mrs Birmingham, host and hostess of the Lord Warden Hotel, are my much esteemed friends, but they are too conceited about the comforts of that establishment when the Night Mail is starting. I know it is a good house to stay at, and I don't want the fact insisted upon in all its warm bright windows at such an hour. I know the Warden is a stationary edifice that never rolls or pitches, and I object to its big outline seeming to insist upon that circumstance, and, as it were, to come over me with it, when I am reeling on the deck of the boat. Beshrew the Warden likewise for obstructing that corner, and making the wind so angry as it rushes round. Shall I not know that it blows quite soon enough, without the officious Warden's interference?

As I wait here on board the night packet, for the South-Eastern Train to come down with the Mail, Dover appears to me to be illuminated for some intensely aggravating festivity in my personal dishonour. All its noises smack of taunting praises of the land, and dispraises of the gloomy sea, and of me for going on it. The drums upon the heights have gone to bed, or I know they would rattle taunts against me for having my unsteady footing on this slippery deck. The many gas eyes of the Marine Parade twinkle in an offensive manner, as if with derision. The distant dogs of Dover bark at me in my mis-shapen wrappers, as if I were Richard the Third.

A screech, a bell, and two red eyes come gliding down the Admiralty Pier with a smoothness of motion rendered more smooth by the heaving of the boat. The sea makes noises against the pier, as if several hippopotami were lapping at it, and were prevented by circumstances over which they had no control from drinking peaceably. We, the boat, become violently agitated – rumble, hum, scream, roar, and establish an immense family washing-day at each paddle-box. Bright patches break out in the train as the doors of the post-office vans are opened, and instantly stooping figures with sacks upon their backs begin to be beheld among the piles, descending as it would seem in ghostly procession to Davy Jones's Locker. The passengers come on board; a few shadowy Frenchmen, with hatboxes shaped like the stoppers of gigantic case-bottles; a few shadowy Germans in immense fur coats and boots; a few shadowy Englishmen prepared for the worst and pretending not to expect it. I cannot disguise from my uncommercial mind the miserable fact that we are a body of outcasts; that the attendants on us are as scant in number as may serve to get rid of us with the least possible delay; that there are no night-loungers interested in us; that the unwilling lamps shiver and shudder at us; that the sole object is to commit us to the deep and abandon us. Lo, the two red eyes glaring in increasing distance, and then the very train itself has gone to bed before we are off!

What is the moral support derived by some sea-going amateurs from an umbrella? Why do certain voyagers across the Channel always put up that article, and hold it up with a grim and fierce tenacity? A fellow-creature near me – whom I only know to *be* a fellow-creature, because of his umbrella: without which he might be a dark bit of cliff, pier, or bulkhead – clutches that instrument with a desperate grasp, that will not relax until he lands at Calais. Is there any analogy, in certain constitutions, between keeping an umbrella up, and keeping the spirits up? A hawser thrown on board with a flop replies 'Stand by!' 'Stand by, below!' 'Half a turn a head!' 'Half a turn a head!' 'Half speed!' 'Half speed!' 'Port!' 'Port!' 'Steady!' 'Steady!' 'Go on!' 'Go on!'

A stout wooden wedge driven in at my right temple and out at my left, a floating deposit of lukewarm oil in my throat, and a compression of the bridge of my nose in a blunt pair of pincers, – these are the personal sensations by which I know we are off, and by which I shall continue to know it until I am on the soil of France. My symptoms have scarcely established themselves comfortably, when two or three skating shadows that have been trying to walk or stand, get flung together, and other two or three shadows in tarpaulin slide with them into corners and cover them up. Then the South Foreland lights begin to hiccup at us in a way that bodes no good.

It is at about this period that my detestation of Calais knows no bounds. Inwardly I resolve afresh that I never will forgive that hated town. I have done so before, many times, but that is past. Let me register a vow. Implacable animosity to Calais everm—— that was an awkward sea, and the funnel seems of my opinion, for it gives a complaining roar.

The wind blows stiffly from the Nor'-East, the sea runs high, we ship a deal of water, the night is dark and cold, and the shapeless passengers lie about in melancholy bundles, as if they were sorted out for the laundress; but for my own uncommercial part I cannot pretend that I am much inconvenienced by any of these things. A general howling whistling flopping gurgling and scooping, I am aware of, and a general knocking about of Nature; but the impressions I receive are very vague. In a sweet faint temper, something like the smell of damaged oranges, I think I should feel languidly benevolent if I had time. I have not time, because I am under a curious compulsion to occupy myself with the Irish melodies. 'Rich and rare were the gems she wore,' is the particular melody to which I find myself devoted. I sing it to myself in the most charming manner and with the greatest expression. Now and then, I raise my head (I am sitting on the hardest of wet seats, in the most uncomfortable of wet attitudes, but I don't mind it,) and notice that I am a whirling shuttle-cock between a fiery battledore of a lighthouse on the French coast and a fiery battledore of a lighthouse on the English coast; but I don't notice it particularly, except to feel envenomed in my hatred of Calais. Then I go on again, 'Rich and rare were the ge-ems she-e-e-e wore, And a bright gold ring on her wa-and she bo-ore, But O her beauty was fa-a-a-a-r beyond' – I am particularly proud of my execution here, when I become aware of another awkward shock from the sea, and another protest from the funnel, and a fellow-creature at the paddle-box more audibly indisposed than I think he need be – 'Her sparkling gems, or snow-white wand, But O her beauty was fa-a-a-a-a-r beyond' – another awkward one here, and the fellow-creature with the umbrella down and picked up – 'Her spa-a-rkling ge-ems, or her Port! port! steady! steady! snow-white fellow-creature at the paddle-box very selfishly audible, bump roar wash white wand.'

As my execution of the Irish melodies partakes of my imperfect perceptions of what is going on around me, so what is going on around me becomes something else than what it is. The stokers open the furnace doors below, to feed the fires, and I am again on the box of the old Exeter Telegraph fast coach, and that is the light of the for ever extinguished coach-lamps, and the gleam on the hatches and paddle-boxes is *their* gleam on cottages and haystacks, and the monotonous noise of the engines is the steady jingle of the splendid team. Anon, the intermittent funnel roar of protest at every violent roll, becomes the regular blast of a high pressure engine, and I recognise the exceedingly explosive steamer in which I ascended the Mississippi when the American civil war was not, and when only its causes were. A fragment of mast on which the light of a lantern falls, an end of rope, and a jerking block or so, become suggestive of Franconi's Circus at Paris where I shall be this very night mayhap (for it must be morning now), and they dance to the self-same time and tune as the trained steed, Black Raven. What may be the speciality of these waves as they come rushing on, I cannot desert the pressing demands made upon me by the gems she wore, to inquire, but they are charged with something about Robinson Crusoe, and I think it was in Yarmouth Roads that he first went a seafaring and was near foundering (what a terrific sound that word had for me when I was a boy!) in his first gale of wind. Still, through all this, I must ask her (who *was* she, I wonder!) for the fiftieth time, and without ever stopping, Does she not fear to stray, So lone and lovely through this bleak way, And are Erin's sons so good or so cold, As not to be tempted by more fellow-creatures at the paddle-box or gold? Sir Knight I feel not the least alarm,

No son of Erin will offer me harm, For though they love fellow-creature with umbrella down again and golden store, Sir Knight they what a tremendous one love honour and virtue more: For though they love Stewards with a bull's eye bright, they'll trouble you for your ticket, sir – rough passage to-night!

I freely admit it to be a miserable piece of human weakness and inconsistency, but I no sooner become conscious of those last words from the steward than I begin to soften towards Calais. Whereas I have been vindictively wishing that those Calais burghers who came out of their town by a short cut into the History of England, with those fatal ropes round their necks by which they have since been towed into so many cartoons, had all been hanged on the spot, I now begin to regard them as highly respectable and virtuous tradesmen. Looking about me, I see the light of Cape Grinez well astern of the boat on the davits to leeward, and the light of Calais Harbour undeniably at its old tricks, but still ahead and shining. Sentiments of forgiveness of Calais, not to say of attachment of Calais, begin to expand my bosom. I have weak notions that I will stay there a day or two on my way back. A faded and recumbent stranger pausing in a profound reverie over the rim of a basin, asked me what kind of place Calais is? I tell him (Heaven forgive me!) a very agreeable place indeed – rather hilly than otherwise.

So strangely goes the time, and on the whole so quickly – though still I seem to have been on board a week – that I am bumped rolled gurgled washed and pitched into Calais Harbour before her maiden smile has finally lighted her through the Green Isle, When blest for ever is she who relied, On entering Calais at the top of the tide. For we have not to land to-night down among those slimy timbers – covered with green hair as if it were the mermaids' favourite combing-place – where one crawls to the surface of the jetty, like a stranded shrimp, but we go steaming up the harbour to the Railway Station Quay. And as we go, the sea washes in and out among piles and planks, with dead heavy beats and in quite a furious manner (whereof we are proud), and the lamps shake in the wind, and the bells of Calais striking One seem to send their vibrations struggling against troubled air, as we have come struggling against troubled water. And now, in the sudden relief and wiping of faces, everybody on board seems to have had a prodigious double-tooth out, and to be this very instant free of the Dentist's hands. And now we all know for the first time how wet and cold we are, and how salt we are; and now I love Calais with my heart of hearts!

'Hôtel Dessin!' (but in this one case it is not a vocal cry; it is but a bright lustre in the eyes of the cheery representative of that best of inns). 'Hôtel Meurice!' 'Hôtel de France!' 'Hôtel de Calais!' 'The Royal Hôtel, Sir, Angaishe ouse!' 'You going to Parry, Sir?' 'Your baggage, registair froo, Sir?' Bless ye, my Touters, bless ye, my commissionaires, bless ye, my hungry-eyed mysteries in caps of a military form, who are always here, day or night, fair weather or foul, seeking inscrutable jobs which I never see you get! Bless ye, my Custom House officers in green and grey; permit me to grasp the welcome hands that descend into my travelling-bag, one on each side, and meet at the bottom to give my change of linen a peculiar shake up, as if it were a measure of chaff or grain! I have nothing to declare, Monsieur le Douanier, except that when I cease to breathe, Calais will be found written on my heart. No article liable to local duty have I with me, Monsieur l'Officier de l'Octroi, unless the overflowing of a breast devoted to your charming town should be in that wise chargeable. Ah! see at the gangway by the twinkling lantern, my dearest brother and friend, he once of the Passport Office, he who collects the names! May he be for ever changeless in his buttoned black surtout, with his note-book in his hand, and his tall black hat surmounting his round smiling patient face! Let us embrace, my dearest brother. I am yours à tout jamais – for the whole of ever.

Calais up and doing at the railway station, and Calais down and dreaming in its bed; Calais with something of 'an ancient and fish-like smell' about it, and Calais blown and sea-washed pure; Calais represented at the Buffet by savoury roast fowls, hot coffee, cognac, and Bordeaux; and Calais represented everywhere by flitting persons with a monomania for changing money – though I never shall be able to understand in my present state

Crossing to Boulogne

of existence how they live by it, but I suppose I should, if I understood the currency question – Calais *en gros*, and Calais *en détail*, forgive one who has deeply wronged you. – I was not fully aware of it on the other side, but I meant Dover.

Ding, ding! To the carriages, gentlemen the travellers. Ascend then, gentlemen the travellers, for Hazebroucke, Lille, Douai, Bruxelles, Arras, Amiens, and Paris! I, humble representative of the uncommercial interest, ascend with the rest. The train is light to-night, and I share my compartment with but two fellow-travellers; one, a compatriot in an obsolete cravat, who thinks it a quite unaccountable thing that they don't keep 'London time' on a French railway, and who is made angry by my modestly suggesting the possibility of Paris time being more in their way; the other, a young priest, with a very small bird in a very small cage, who feeds the small bird with a quill, and then puts him up in the network above his head, where he advances twittering, to his front wires, and seems to address me in an electioneering manner. The compatriot (who crossed in the boat, and whom I judge to be some person of distinction, as he was shut up, like a stately species of rabbit, in a private hutch on deck) and the young priest (who joined us at Calais) are soon asleep, and then the bird and I have it all to ourselves.

A stormy night still; a night that sweeps the wires of the electric telegraph with a wild and fitful hand; a night so very stormy, with the added storm of the train-progress through it, that when the Guard comes clambering round to mark the tickets while we are at full speed (a really horrible performance in an express train, though he holds on to the open window by his elbows in the most deliberate manner), he stands in such a whirlwind that I grip him fast by the collar, and feel it next to manslaughter to let him go. Still, when he is gone, the small small bird remains at his front wires feebly twittering to me – twittering and twittering, until, leaning back in my place and looking at him in drowsy fascination, I find that he seems to jog my memory as we rush along.

Uncommercial travels (thus the small small bird) have lain in their idle thriftless way through all this range of swamp and dyke, as through many other odd places; and about here, as you very well know, are the queer old stone farmhouses, approached by drawbridges, and the windmills that you get at by boats. Here, are the lands where the women hoe and dig, paddling canoe-wise from field to field, and here are the cabarets and other peasant-houses where the stone dove-cotes in the littered yards are as strong as warders' towers in old castles. Here, are the long monotonous miles of canal, with the great Dutch-built barges garishly painted, and the towing girls, sometimes harnessed by the forehead, sometimes by the girdle and the shoulders, not a pleasant sight to see. Scattered through this country are mighty works of VAUBAN, whom you know about, and regiments of such corporals as you heard of once upon a time, and many a blue-eyed Bebelle. Through these flat districts, in the shining summer days, walk those long grotesque files of young novices in enormous shovel-hats, whom you remember blackening the ground checkered by the avenues of leafy trees. And now that Hazebroucke slumbers certain kilometres ahead, recall the summer evening when your dusty feet strolling up from the station tended hap-hazard to a Fair there, where the oldest inhabitants were circling round and round a barrel-organ on hobby-horses, with the greatest gravity, and where the principal show in the Fair was a Religious Richardson's – literally, on its own announcement in great letters, THEATRE RELIGIEUX. In which improving Temple, the dramatic representation was of 'all the interesting events in the life of our Lord, from the Manger to the Tomb;' the principal female character, without any reservation or exception, being at the moment of your arrival, engaged in trimming the external Moderators (as it was growing dusk), while the next principal female character took the money, and the Young Saint John disported himself upside down on the platform.

Looking up at this point to confirm the small small bird in every particular he has mentioned, I find he has ceased to twitter, and has put his head under his wing. Therefore, in my different way I follow the good example.

The first visit to Italy

It was seven years before Dickens crossed the Channel again, although he and Catherine had made a horrific voyage across the Atlantic and back when they visited America in 1841, leaving their four children in the care of Mrs Macready, the actor's wife, helped by Georgina Hogarth, Catherine's sister, who thereafter became a permanent member of the household. Now, in 1844, worn out by eight years in which he had written Sketches by Boz, Pickwick Papers, Oliver Twist, Master Humphrey's Clock, The Old Curiosity Shop, Barnaby Rudge, American Notes, Martin Chuzzlewit *and* A Christmas Carol, *Dickens decided to leave England for a year, this time taking the whole family which now included a fifth baby. Having let his London house and engaged one in Albaro, a suburb of Genoa, he bought, for forty-five pounds, a great lumbering family coach in which to transport them from Calais to Marseilles. He was most fortunate in securing, as courier and general factotum, Louis Roche, a native of Avignon generally referred to as 'The Brave', a charming as well as most efficient servant. He was to pilot Dickens through many later journeys, but died in 1849 of heart disease.*

As soon as he had settled in Genoa, Dickens began sending to Forster week by week those impressions and descriptive pieces which were later published as Pictures from Italy. *The first chapter gives a factual, though still 'Dickensian', account of that coach-journey through France.*

GOING THROUGH FRANCE

On a fine Sunday morning in the Midsummer time and weather of eighteen hundred and forty-four, it was, my good friend, when – don't be alarmed; not when two travellers might have been observed slowly making their way over that picturesque and broken ground by which the first chapter of a Middle-Aged novel is usually attained – but when an English travelling-carriage of considerable proportions, fresh from the shady halls of the Pantechnicon near Belgrave Square, London, was observed (by a very small French soldier; for I saw him look at it) to issue from the gate of the Hôtel Meurice in the Rue Rivoli at Paris.

I am no more bound to explain why the English family travelling by this carriage, inside and out, should be starting for Italy on a Sunday morning, of all good days in the week, than I am to assign a reason for all the little men in France being soldiers, and all the big men postillions; which is the invariable rule. But, they had some sort of reason for what they did, I have no doubt; and their reason for being there at all, was, as you know, that they were going to live in fair Genoa for a year; and that the head of the family purposed, in that space of time, to stroll about, wherever his restless humour carried him.

And it would have been small comfort to me to have explained to the population of Paris generally, that I was that Head and Chief; and not the radiant embodiment of good humour who sat beside me in the person of a French Courier – best of servants and most beaming of men! Truth to say, he looked a great deal more patriarchal than I, who, in the shadow of his portly presence, dwindled down to no account at all.

There was, of course, very little in the aspect of Paris – as we rattled near the dismal Morgue and over the Pont Neuf – to reproach us for our Sunday travelling. The wineshops (every second house) were driving a roaring trade; awnings were spreading, and chairs and tables arranging, outside the cafés, preparatory to the eating of ices, and drinking of cool liquids, later in the day; shoeblacks were busy on the bridges; shops were open; carts and waggons clattered to and fro; the narrow, up-hill, funnel-like streets across the River, were so many dense perspectives of crowd and bustle, parti-coloured nightcaps, tobacco-pipes, blouses, large boots, and shaggy heads of hair; nothing at that hour denoted a day of rest, unless it were the appearance, here and there, of a family pleasure-party, crammed

Approaching Abbeville

into a bulky old lumbering cab; or of some contemplative holiday-maker in the freest and easiest dishabille, leaning out of a low garret window, watching the drying of his newly polished shoes on the little parapet outside (if a gentleman), or the airing of her stockings in the sun (if a lady), with calm anticipation.

Once clear of the never-to-be-forgotten-or-forgiven pavement which surrounds Paris, the first three days of travelling towards Marseilles are quiet and monotonous enough. To Sens. To Avallon. To Chalons. A sketch of one day's proceedings is a sketch of all three; and here it is.

We have four horses, and one postillion, who has a very long whip, and drives his team, something like the Courier of Saint Petersburg in the circle at Astley's or Franconi's: only he sits his own horse instead of standing on him. The immense jack-boots worn by these postillions, are sometimes a century or two old; and are so ludicrously disproportionate to the wearer's foot, that the spur, which is put where his own heel comes, is generally halfway up the leg of the boots. The man often comes out of the stable-yard, with his whip in his hand and his shoes on, and brings out, in both hands, one boot at a time, which he plants on the ground by the side of his horse, with great gravity, until everything is ready. When it is – and oh Heaven! the noise they make about it! – he gets into the boots, shoes and all, or is hoisted into them by a couple of friends; adjusts the rope harness, embossed by the labours of innumerable pigeons in the stables; makes all the horses kick and plunge; cracks his whip like a madman; shouts 'En route – Hi!' and away we go. He is sure to have a contest with his horse before we have gone very far; and then he calls him a Thief, and a Brigand, and a Pig, and what not; and beats him about the head as if he were made of wood.

There is little more than one variety in the appearance of the country, for the first two days. From a dreary plain, to an interminable avenue, and from an interminable avenue to a dreary plain again. Plenty of vines there are in the open fields, but of a short low kind, and not trained in festoons, but about straight sticks. Beggars innumerable there are, everywhere; but an extraordinarily scanty population, and fewer children than I ever encountered. I don't believe we saw a hundred children between Paris and Chalons. Queer old towns, drawbridged and walled: with odd little towers at the angles, like grotesque faces, as if the wall had put a mask on, and were staring down into the moat; other strange little towers, in gardens and fields, and down lanes, and in farm-yards: all alone, and always round, with a peaked roof, and never used for any purpose at all; ruinous buildings of all sorts; sometimes an hôtel de ville, sometimes a guard-house, sometimes a dwelling-house, sometimes a château with a rank garden, prolific in dandelion, and watched over by extinguisher-topped turrets, and blink-eyed little casements; are the standard objects, repeated over and over again. Sometimes we pass a village inn, with a crumbling wall belonging to it, and a perfect town of out-houses; and painted over the gateway, 'Stabling for Sixty Horses;' as indeed there might be stabling for sixty score, were there any horses to be stabled there, or anybody resting there, or anything stirring about the place but a dangling bush, indicative of the wine inside: which flutters idly in the wind, in lazy keeping with everything else, and certainly is never in a green old age, though always so old as to be dropping to pieces. And all day long, strange little narrow waggons, in strings of six or eight, bringing cheese from Switzerland, and frequently in charge, the whole line, of one man, or even boy – and he very often asleep in the foremost cart – come jingling past: the horses drowsily ringing the bells upon their harness, and looking as if they thought (no doubt they do) their great blue woolly furniture, of immense weight and thickness, with a pair of grotesque horns growing out of the collar, very much too warm for the Midsummer weather.

Then, there is the Diligence, twice or thrice a-day; with the dusty outsides in blue frocks, like butchers; and the insides in white nightcaps; and its cabriolet head on the roof, nodding and shaking, like an idiot's head; and its Young-France passengers staring out of window, with beards down to their waists, and blue spectacles awfully shading their warlike eyes, and very big sticks clenched in their National grasp. Also the Malle Poste, with only a couple of passengers, tearing along at a real good dare-devil pace, and out of sight in no time. Steady old Curés come jolting past, now and then, in such ramshackle, rusty, musty, clattering coaches as no Englishman would believe in; and bony women dawdle about in solitary places, holding cows by ropes while they feed, or digging and hoeing or doing field-work of a more laborious kind, or representing real shepherdesses with their flocks – to obtain an adequate idea of which pursuit and its followers, in any country, it is only necessary to take any pastoral poem, or picture, and imagine to yourself whatever is most exquisitely and widely unlike the descriptions therein contained.

You have been travelling along, stupidly enough, as you generally do in the last stage of the day; and the ninety-six bells upon the horses – twenty-four apiece – have been ringing sleepily in your ears for half an hour or so; and it has become a very jog-trot, monotonous, tiresome sort of business; and you have been thinking deeply about the dinner you will have at the next stage; when, down at the end of the long avenue of trees through which you are travelling, the first indication of a town appears, in the shape of some straggling cottages: and the carriage begins to rattle and roll over a horribly uneven pavement. As if the equipage were a great firework, and the mere sight of a smoking cottage chimney had lighted it, instantly it begins to crack and splutter, as if the very devil were in it. Crack, crack, crack, crack. Crack-crack-crack. Crick-crack. Crick-crack. Helo! Hola! Vite! Voleur! Brigand! Hi hi hi! En r-r-r-r-r-route! Whip, wheels, driver, stones, beggars, children, crack, crack, crack; helo! hola! charité pour l'amour de Dieu! crick-crack-crick-crack; crick, crick, crick; bump, jolt, crack, bump, crick-crack; round the corner, up the narrow street, down the paved hill on the other side; in the gutter; bump, bump; jolt, jog, crick, crick, crick; crack, crack, crack; into the shop-windows on the left-hand side of the street, preliminary to a sweeping turn into the wooden archway on the right; rumble, rumble, rumble; clatter, clatter, clatter; crick, crick, crick; and here we are in the yard of the Hôtel de l'Ecu d'Or; used up, gone out, smoking, spent, exhausted; but sometimes making a false start unexpectedly, with nothing coming of it – like a firework to the last!

The landlady of the Hôtel de l'Ecu d'Or is here; and the landlord of the Hôtel de l'Ecu d'Or is here; and the femme de chambre of the Hôtel de l'Ecu d'Or is here; and a gentleman in a glazed cap, with a red beard like a bosom friend, who is staying at the Hôtel de l'Ecu d'Or, is here; and Monsieur le Curé is walking up and down in a corner of the yard by himself, with a shovel hat upon his head, and a black gown on his back, and a book in one hand, and an umbrella in the other; and everybody, except Monsieur le Curé, is open-mouthed and open-eyed, for the opening of the carriage-door. The landlord of the Hôtel de l'Ecu d'Or, dotes to that extent upon the Courier, that he can hardly wait for his coming down from the box, but embraces his very legs and boot-heels as he descends. 'My Courier! My brave Courier! My friend! My brother!' The landlady loves him, the femme de chambre blesses him, the garçon worships him. The Courier asks if his letter has been received? It has, it has. Are the rooms prepared? They are, they are. The best rooms for my noble Courier. The rooms of state for my gallant Courier; the whole house is at the service of my best of friends! He keeps his hand upon the carriage-door, and asks some other question to enhance the expectation. He carries a green leathern purse outside his coat, suspended by a belt. The idlers look at it; one touches it. It is full of five-franc pieces. Murmurs of admiration are heard among the boys. The landlord falls upon the Courier's neck, and folds him to his breast. He is so much fatter than he was, he says! He looks so rosy and so well!

The door is opened. Breathless expectation. The lady of the family gets out. Ah sweet lady! Beautiful lady! The sister of the lady of the family gets out. Great Heaven, Ma'amselle is charming! First little boy gets out. Ah, what a beautiful little boy! First little girl gets out. Oh, but this is an enchanting child! Second little girl gets out. The landlady, yielding to the finest impulse of our common nature, catches her up in her arms! Second little boy gets out. Oh, the sweet boy! Oh, the tender little family! The baby is handed out. Angelic baby! The baby has topped everything. All the rapture is expended on the baby!

Then the two nurses tumble out; and the enthusiasm swelling into madness, the whole family are swept upstairs as on a cloud; while the idlers press about the carriage, and look into it, and walk round it, and touch it. For it is something to touch a carriage that has held so many people. It is a legacy to leave one's children.

The rooms are on the first floor, except the nursery for the night, which is a great rambling chamber, with four or five beds in it: through a dark passage, up two steps, down four, past a pump, across a balcony, and next door to the stable. The other sleeping apartments are large and lofty; each with two small bedsteads, tastefully hung, like the windows, with red and white drapery. The sitting-room is famous. Dinner is already laid in it for three; and the napkins are folded in cocked-hat fashion. The floors are of red tile. There are no carpets, and not much furniture to speak of; but there is abundance of looking-glass, and there are large vases under glass shades, filled with artificial flowers; and there are plenty of clocks. The whole party are in motion. The brave Courier, in particular, is everywhere: looking after the beds, having wine poured down his throat by his dear brother the landlord, and picking up green cucumbers – always cucumbers; Heaven knows where he gets them – with which he walks about, one in each hand, like truncheons.

Dinner is announced. There is very thin soup; there are very large loaves – one apiece; a fish; four dishes afterwards; some poultry afterwards; a dessert afterwards; and no lack of wine. There is not much in the dishes; but they are very good, and always ready instantly. When it is nearly dark, the brave Courier, having eaten the two cucumbers, sliced up in the contents of a pretty large decanter of oil, and another of vinegar, emerges from his retreat below, and proposes a visit to the Cathedral, whose massive tower frowns down upon the court-yard of the inn. Off we go; and very solemn and grand it is, in the dim light: so dim at last, that the polite, old, lantern-jawed Sacristan has a feeble little bit of candle in his hand, to grope among the tombs with – and looks among the grim columns, very like a lost ghost who is searching for his own.

Underneath the balcony, when we return, the inferior servants of the inn are supping in the open air, at a great table; the dish, a stew of meat and vegetables, smoking hot, and served in the iron cauldron it was boiled in. They have a pitcher of thin wine, and are very merry; merrier than the gentleman with the red beard, who is playing billiards in the light room on the left of the yard, where shadows, with cues in their hands, and cigars in their mouths, cross and recross the window, constantly. Still the thin Curé walks up and down alone, with his book and umbrella. And there he walks, and there the billiard-balls rattle, long after we are fast asleep.

We are astir at six next morning. It is a delightful day, shaming yesterday's mud upon the carriage, if anything could shame a carriage, in a land where carriages are never cleaned. Everybody is brisk; and as we finish breakfast, the horses come jingling into the yard from the Post-house. Everything taken out of the carriage is put back again. The brave Courier announces that all is ready, after walking into every room, and looking all round it, to be certain that nothing is left behind. Everybody gets in. Everybody connected with the Hôtel de l'Ecu d'Or is again enchanted. The brave Courier runs into the house for a parcel containing cold fowl, sliced ham, bread, and biscuits, for lunch; hands it into the coach; and runs back again.

What has he got in his hand now? More cucumbers? No. A long strip of paper. It's the bill.

The brave Courier has two belts on, this morning: one supporting the purse: another, a mighty good sort of leathern bottle, filled to the throat with the best light Bordeaux wine in the house. He never pays the bill till this bottle is full. Then he disputes it.

He disputes it now, violently. He is still the landlord's brother, but by another father or mother. He is not so nearly related to him as he was last night. The landlord scratches his head. The brave Courier points to certain figures in the bill, and intimates that if they remain there, the Hôtel de l'Ecu d'Or is thenceforth and for ever an hôtel de l'Ecu de cuivre. The landlord goes into a little counting-house. The brave Courier follows, forces the bill and a pen into his hand, and talks more rapidly than ever. The landlord takes the pen. The Courier smiles. The landlord makes an alteration. The Courier cuts a joke. The landlord is affectionate, but not weakly so. He bears it like a man. He shakes hands with his brave brother; but he don't hug him. Still, he loves his brother; for he knows that he will be returning that way, one of these fine days, with another family, and he foresees that his heart will yearn towards him again. The brave Courier traverses all round the carriage once, looks at the drag, inspects the wheels, jumps up, gives the word, and away we go!

It is market morning. The market is held in the little square outside in front of the cathedral. It is crowded with men and women, in blue, in red, in green, in white; with canvased stalls; and fluttering merchandise. The country people are grouped about, with their clean baskets before them. Here, the lace-sellers; there, the butter and egg-sellers; there, the fruit-sellers; there, the shoemakers. The whole place looks as if it were the stage of some great theatre, and the curtain had just run up, for a picturesque ballet. And there is the cathedral to boot: scene-like: all grim, and swarthy, and mouldering, and cold; just splashing the pavement in one place with faint purple drops, as the morning sun, entering by a little window on the eastern side, struggles through some stained glass panes, on the western.

In five minutes we have passed the iron cross, with a little ragged kneeling-place of turf before it, in the outskirts of the town; and are again upon the road.

Genoa

Two of the most congenial friends of this period, to whom Dickens remained devoted for the rest of their lives, were the distinguished artists Daniel Maclise and Clarkson Stanfield, and it was to Maclise that, on 22 July 1844, he wrote from Genoa a sparkling letter that reveals his intense appreciation of natural beauty.

FIRST RAPTURES

I address you with something of the lofty spirit of an exile – a banished commoner – a sort of Anglo-Pole. I don't exactly know what I have done for my country in coming away from it; but I feel it is something – something great – something virtuous and heroic. Lofty emotions rise within me, when I see the sun set on the blue Mediterranean. I am the limpet on the rock. My father's name is Turner, and my boots are green.

Apropos of blue. In a certain picture, called 'The Serenade', you painted a sky. If you ever have occasion to paint the Mediterranean, let it be exactly of that colour. It lies before me now, as deeply and intensely blue. But no such colour is above me. Nothing like it. In the South of France – at Avignon, at Aix, at Marseilles – I saw deep blue skies (not *so* deep though – oh Lord, no!), and also in America; but the sky above me is familiar to my sight. Is it heresy to say that I have seen its twin-brother shining through the window of Jack Straw's – that down in Devonshire I have seen a better sky? I daresay it is; but like a great many other heresies, it is true.

But such green – green – green – as flutters in the vineyard down below the windows, *that* I never saw; nor yet such lilac, and such purple as float between me and the distant hills; nor

Genoa

yet – in anything – picture, book, or verbal boredom – such awful, solemn, impenetrable blue, as is that same sea. It has such an absorbing, silent, deep, profound effect, that I can't help thinking it suggested the idea of Styx. It looks as if a draught of it – only so much as you could scoop up on the beach, in the hollow of your hand – would wash out everything else, and make a great blue blank of your intellect.

When the sun sets clearly, then, by Heaven, it is majestic! From any one of eleven windows here, or from a terrace overgrown with grapes, you may behold the broad sea; villas, houses, mountains, forts, strewn with rose leaves – strewn with thorns – stifled in thorns! Dyed through and through and through. For a moment. No more. The sun is impatient and fierce, like everything else in these parts, and goes down headlong. Run to fetch your hat – and it's night. Wink at the right time of black night – and it's morning. Everything is in extremes. There is an insect here (I forget its name, and Fletcher and Roche are both out) that chirps all day. There is one outside the window now. The chirp is very loud, something like a Brobdingnagian grasshopper. The creature is born to chirp – to progress in chirping – to chirp louder, louder, louder – till it gives one tremendous chirp, and bursts itself. That is its life and death. Everything 'is in a concatenation accordingly.' The day gets brighter, brighter, brighter, till it's night. The summer gets hotter, hotter, hotter, till it bursts. The fruit gets riper, riper, riper, till it tumbles down and rots.

Ask me a question or two about fresco – will you be so good? All the houses are painted in fresco hereabout – the outside walls I mean; the fronts, and backs, and sides – and all the colour has run into damp and green seediness, and the very design has struggled away into the component atoms of the plaster. Sometimes (but not often) I can make out a Virgin with a mildewed glory round her head; holding nothing, in an indiscernible lap, with invisible arms; and occasionally the leg or arms of a cherub, but it is very melancholy and dim. There are two old fresco-painted vases outside my own gate – one on either hand – which are so faint, that I never saw them till last night; and only then because I was looking over the wall after a lizard, who had come upon me while I was smoking a cigar above, and crawled over one of these embellishments to his retreat. There is a church here – the Church of the Annunciation – which they are now (by 'they' I mean certain noble families) restoring at a vast expense, as a work of piety. It is a large church, with a great many little chapels in it, and a very high dome. Every inch of this edifice is painted, and every design is set in a great gold frame or border elaborately wrought. You can imagine nothing so splendid. It is worth coming the whole distance to see. But every sort of splendour is in perpetual enactment through the means of these churches. Gorgeous processions in the streets, illuminations of windows on festa nights; lighting up of lamps and clustering of flowers before the shrines of saints; all manner of show and display. The doors of the churches stand wide open; and in this hot weather great red curtains flutter and wave in their palaces; and if you go and sit in one of these to get out of the sun, you see the queerest figures kneeling against pillars, and the strangest people passing in and out, and vast streams of women in veils (they don't wear bonnets), with great fans in their hands, coming and going, that you are never tired of looking on. Except in the churches, you would suppose the city (at this time of year) to be deserted, the people keep so close within doors. Indeed it is next to impossible to go out into the heat. I have only been into Genoa twice myself. We are deliciously cool here, by comparison; being high, and having the sea breeze. There is always some shade in the vineyard, too; and underneath the rocks on the seashore, so if I choose to saunter I can do it easily, even in the hot time of the day. I am as lazy, however, as – as you are, and do little but eat and drink and read.

As I am going to transmit regular accounts of all sight-seeings and journeyings to Forster, who will show them to you, I will not bore you with descriptions, however. I hardly think you allow enough for the great brightness and brilliancy of colour which is commonly achieved on the Continent, in that same fresco painting. I saw some – by a French artist and his pupil – in progress at the cathedral at Avignon, which was as bright and airy as anything can be, – nothing dull or dead about it; and I have observed quite fierce and glaring colours elsewhere.

We have a piano now (there was none in the house), and have fallen into a pretty settled easy track. We breakfast about half-past nine or ten, dine about four, and go to bed about eleven. We are much courted by the visiting people, of course, and I very much resort to my old habit of bolting from callers, and leaving their reception to Kate. Green figs I have already learnt to like. Green almonds (we have them at dessert every day) are the most delicious fruit in the world. And green lemons, combined with some rare hollands that is to be got here, make prodigious punch, I assure you. You ought to come over, Mac; but I don't expect you, though I am sure it would be a very good move for you. I have not the smallest doubt of that. Fletcher has made a sketch of the house, and will copy it in pen-and-ink for transmission to you in my next letter. I shall look out for a place in Genoa, between this and the winter time. In the meantime, the people who come out here breathe delightedly, as if they had got into another climate. Landing in the city, you would hardly suppose it possible that there could be such an air within two miles.

Write to me as often as you can, like a dear good fellow, and rely upon the punctuality of my correspondence. Losing you and Forster is like losing my arms and legs, and dull and lame I am without you. But at Broadstairs next year, please God, when it is all over, I shall be very glad to have laid up such a store of recollections and improvement.

I don't know what to do with Timber. He is as ill-adapted to the climate at this time of year as a suit of fur. I have had him made a lion dog; but the fleas flock in such crowds into the hair he has left, that they drive him nearly frantic, and renders it absolutely necessary that he should be kept by himself. Of all the miserable hideous little frights you ever saw, you never beheld such a devil. Apropos, as we were crossing the Seine within two stages of Paris, Roche suddenly said to me, sitting by me on the box: 'The littel dog 'ave got a great lip!' I was thinking of things remote and very different, and couldn't comprehend why any peculiarity in this feature on the part of the dog should excite a man so much. As I was musing upon it, my ears were attracted by shouts of 'Helo! hola! Hi, hi, hi! Le voilà! Regardez!' and the like. And looking down among the oxen – we were in the centre of a numerous drove – I saw him, Timber, lying in the road, curled up – you know his way – like a lobster, only not so stiff, yelping dismally in the pain of his 'lip' from the roof of the carriage; and between the aching of his bones, his horror of the oxen, and his dread of me (who he evidently took to be the immediate agent in and cause of the damage), singing out to an extent which I believe to be perfectly unprecedented; while every Frenchman and French boy within sight roared for company. He wasn't hurt.

Kate and Georgina send their best loves; and the children add 'theirs.' Katey, in particular, desires to be commended to 'Mr Teese.' She has a sore throat; from sitting in constant draughts, I suppose; but with that exception, we are all quite well.

But he was not quite so enthusiastic about the house which had been engaged for him by a friend. Indeed, he named it 'The Pink Jail'.

THE PINK JAIL

The first impressions of such a place as ALBARO, the suburb of Genoa, where I am now, as my American friends would say, 'located,' can hardly fail, I should imagine, to be mournful and disappointing. It requires a little time and use to overcome the feeling of depression consequent, at first, on so much ruin and neglect. Novelty, pleasant to most people, is particularly delightful, I think, to me. I am not easily dispirited when I have the means of pursuing my own fancies and occupations; and I believe I have some natural aptitude for accommodating myself to circumstances. But, as yet, I stroll about here, in all the holes and corners of the neighbourhood, in a perpetual state of forlorn surprise; and returning to my villa: the Villa Bagnerello (it sounds romantic, but Signor Bagnerello is a butcher hard by): have sufficient occupation in pondering over my new experiences, and comparing them, very much to my own amusement, with my expectations, until I wander out again.

Villa di Bella Vista at Albaro

The Villa Bagnerello: or the Pink Jail, a far more expressive name for the mansion: is in one of the most splendid situations imaginable. The noble bay of Genoa, with the deep blue Mediterranean, lies stretched out near at hand; monstrous old desolate houses and palaces are dotted all about; lofty hills, with their tops often hidden in the clouds, and with strong forts perched high up on their craggy sides, are close upon the left; and in front, stretching from the walls of the house, down to a ruined chapel which stands upon the bold and picturesque rocks on the sea-shore, are green vineyards, where you may wander all day long in partial shade, through interminable vistas of grapes, trained on a rough trellis-work across the narrow paths.

This sequestered spot is approached by lanes so very narrow, that when we arrived at the Custom-house, we found the people here had *taken the measure* of the narrowest among them, and were waiting to apply it to the carriage; which ceremony was gravely performed in the street, while we all stood by in breathless suspense. It was found to be a very tight fit, but just a possibility, and no more – as I am reminded every day, by the sight of various large holes which it punched in the walls on either side as it came along. We are more fortunate, I am told, than an old lady, who took a house in these parts not long ago, and who stuck fast in *her* carriage in a lane; and as it was impossible to open one of the doors, she was obliged to submit to the indignity of being hauled through one of the little front windows, like a harlequin.

When you have got through these narrow lanes, you come to an archway, imperfectly stopped up by a rusty old gate – my gate. The rusty old gate has a bell to correspond, which you ring as long as you like, and which nobody answers, as it has no connexion whatever with the house. But there is a rusty old knocker, too – very loose, so that it slides round when you touch it – and if you learn the trick of it, and knock long enough, somebody comes. The brave Courier comes, and gives you admittance. You walk into a seedy little garden, all wild and weedy, from which the vineyard opens; cross it, enter a square hall like a cellar, walk up a cracked marble staircase, and pass into a most enormous room with a vaulted roof and whitewashed walls: not unlike a great Methodist chapel. This is the *sala*. It has five windows and five doors, and is decorated with pictures which would gladden the heart of one of those picture-cleaners in London who hang up, as a sign, a picture divided, like death and the lady, at the top of the old ballad: which always leaves you in a state of uncertainty whether the ingenious professor has cleaned one half, or dirtied the other. The furniture of this *sala* is a sort of red brocade. All the chairs are immovable, and the sofa weighs several tons.

On the same floor, and opening out of this same chamber, are dining-room, drawing-room, and divers bed-rooms: each with a multiplicity of doors and windows. Upstairs are divers other gaunt chambers, and a kitchen; and downstairs is another kitchen, which, with all sorts of strange contrivances for burning charcoal, looks like an alchemical laboratory. There are also some half-dozen small sitting-rooms, where the servants in this hot July, may escape from the heat of the fire, and where the brave Courier plays all sorts of musical instruments of his own manufacture, all the evening long. A mighty old, wandering, ghostly, echoing, grim, bare house it is, as ever I beheld or thought of.

There is a little vine-covered terrace, opening from the drawing-room; and under this terrace, and forming one side of the little garden, is what used to be the stable. It is now a cow-house, and has three cows in it, so that we get new milk by the bucketful. There is no pasturage near, and they never go out, but are constantly lying down, and surfeiting themselves with vine-leaves – perfect Italian cows enjoying the *dolce far' niente* all day long. They are presided over, and slept with, by an old man named Antonio, and his son; two burnt-sienna natives with naked legs and feet, who wear, each, a shirt, a pair of trousers, and a red sash, with a relic, or some sacred charm like the bonbon off a twelfth-cake, hanging round the neck. The old man is very anxious to convert me to the Catholic faith, and exhorts me frequently. We sit upon a stone by the door, sometimes in the evening, like Robinson Crusoe and Friday reversed; and he generally relates, towards my conversion, an abridgment of the History of Saint Peter – chiefly, I believe, from the unspeakable delight he has in his imitation of the cock.

The view, as I have said, is charming; but in the day you must keep the lattice-blinds close shut, or the sun would drive you mad; and when the sun goes down you must shut up all the windows, or the mosquitoes would tempt you to commit suicide. So at this time of the year, you don't see much of the prospect within doors. As for the flies, you don't mind them. Nor the fleas, whose size is prodigious, and whose name is Legion, and populate the coach-house to that extent that I daily expect to see the carriage going off bodily, drawn by myriads of industrious fleas in harness. The rats are kept away, quite comfortable, by scores of lean cats, who roam about the garden for that purpose. The lizards, of course, nobody cares for; they play in the sun, and don't bite. The little scorpions are merely curious. The beetles are rather late, and have not appeared yet. The frogs are company. There is a preserve of them in the grounds of the next villa; and after nightfall, one would think that scores upon scores of women in pattens were going up and down a wet stone pavement without a moment's cessation. That is exactly the noise they make.

But Dickens soon began to feel at home in Genoa, and it was not long before Forster was to see in his imagination 'the light, eager, active figure' which was soon to become as familiar in the streets of Genoa as it had been in London. Before he left home, Dickens had taken lessons in Italian, and now he began asking for things in the little shops 'as bold as a lion'. But, he wrote, he was constantly being reminded of London. The broadest streets in Genoa were narrower than Wych Street or Drury Lane. Later on, other Italian cities were to give him the feeling that he must be in Whitechapel or just coming up to the little barber's shop on the way to Holywell Street.

LATER IMPRESSIONS

In the course of two months, the flitting shapes and shadows of my dismal entering reverie gradually resolved themselves into familiar forms and substances; and I already began to think that when the time should come, a year hence, for closing the long holiday and turning back to England, I might part from Genoa with anything but a glad heart.

It is a place that 'grows upon you' every day. There seems to be always something to find out in it. There are the most extraordinary alleys and by-ways to walk about in. You can lose your way (what a comfort that is, when you are idle!) twenty times a day, if you like; and turn up again, under the most unexpected and surprising difficulties. It abounds in the strangest contrasts; things that are picturesque, ugly, mean, magnificent, delightful, and offensive, break upon the view at every turn.

They who would know how beautiful the country immediately surrounding Genoa is, should climb (in clear weather) to the top of Monte Faccio, or, at least, ride round the city walls: a feat more easily performed. No prospect can be more diversified and lovely than the changing views of the harbour, and the valleys of the two rivers, the Polcevera and the Bizagno, from the heights along which the strongly fortified walls are carried, like the great wall of China in little. In not the least picturesque part of this ride, there is a fair specimen of a real Genoese tavern, where the visitor may derive good entertainment from real Genoese dishes, such as Tagliarini; Ravioli; German sausages, strong of garlic, sliced and eaten with fresh green figs; cocks' combs and sheep-kidneys, chopped up with mutton chops and liver; small pieces of some unknown part of a calf, twisted into small shreds, fried, and served up in a great dish like white-bait; and other curiosities of that kind. They often get wine at these surburban Trattorie, from France and Spain and Portugal, which is brought over by small captains in little trading-vessels. They buy it at so much a bottle, without asking what it is, or caring to remember if anybody tells them, and usually divide it into two heaps; of which they label one Champagne, and the other Madeira. The various opposite flavours, qualities, countries, ages, and vintages that are comprised under these two general heads is quite extraordinary. The most limited range is probably from cool Gruel up to old Marsala, and down again to apple Tea.

The great majority of the streets are as narrow as any thoroughfare can well be, where people (even Italian people) are supposed to live and walk about; being mere lanes, with here and there a kind of well, or breathing-place. The houses are immensely high, painted in all sorts of colours, and are in every stage and state of damage, dirt, and lack of repair. They are commonly let off in floors, or flats, like the houses in the old town of Edinburgh, or many houses in Paris. There are few street doors; the entrance halls are, for the most part, looked upon as public property; and any moderately enterprising scavenger might make a fine fortune by now and then clearing them out. As it is impossible for coaches to penetrate into these streets, there are sedan chairs, gilded and otherwise, for hire in divers places. A great many private chairs are also kept among the nobility and gentry; and at night these are trotted to and fro in all directions, preceded by bearers of great lanterns, made of linen stretched upon a frame. The sedans and lanterns are the legitimate successors of the long strings of patient and much-abused mules, that go jingling their little bells through these confined streets all day long. They follow them, as regularly as the stars the sun.

When shall I forget the Streets of Palaces: the Strada Nuova and the Strada Balbi! or how the former looked one summer day, when I first saw it underneath the brightest and most intensely blue of summer skies: which its narrow perspective of immense mansions reduced to a tapering and most precious strip of brightness, looking down upon the heavy shade below! A brightness not too common, even in July and August, to be well esteemed: for, if the Truth must out, there were not eight blue skies in as many midsummer weeks, saving, sometimes, early in the morning; when, looking out to sea, the water and the firmament were one world of deep and brilliant blue. At other times, there were clouds and haze enough to make an Englishman grumble in his own climate.

The endless details of these rich Palaces: the walls of some of them, within, alive with masterpieces by Vandyke! The great, heavy, stone balconies, one above another, and tier over tier:

with here and there, one larger than the rest, towering high up – a huge marble platform; the doorless vestibules, massively barred lower windows, immense public staircases, thick marble pillars, strong dungeon-like arches, and dreary, dreaming, echoing vaulted chambers: among which the eye wanders again, and again, and again, as every palace is succeeded by another – the terrace gardens between house and house, with green arches of the vine, and groves of orange-trees, and blushing oleander in full bloom, twenty, thirty, forty feet above the street – the painted halls, mouldering, and blotting, and rotting in the damp corners, and still shining out in beautiful colours and voluptuous designs, where the walls are dry – the faded figures on the outsides of the houses, holding wreaths, and crowns, and flying upward, and downward, and standing in niches, and here and there looking fainter and more feeble than elsewhere, by contrast with some fresh little Cupids, who on a more recently decorated portion of the front, are stretching out what seems to be the semblance of a blanket, but is, indeed, a sun-dial – the steep, steep, up-hill streets of small palaces (but very large palaces for all that), with marble terraces looking down into close by-ways – the magnificent and innumerable Churches; and the rapid passage from a street of stately edifices, into a maze of the vilest squalor, steaming with unwholesome stenches, and swarming with half-naked children and whole worlds of dirty people – make up, altogether, such a scene of wonder: so lively, and yet so dead: so noisy, and yet so quiet: so obtrusive, and yet so shy and lowering: so wide awake, and yet so fast asleep: that it is a sort of intoxication to a stranger to walk on, and on, and on, and look about him. A bewildering phantasmagoria, with all the inconsistency of a dream, and all the pain and all the pleasure of an extravagant reality!

The different uses to which some of these Palaces are applied, all at once, is characteristic. For instance, the English Banker (my excellent and hospitable friend) had his office in a good-sized Palazzo in the Strada Nuova. In the hall (every inch of which is elaborately painted, but which is as dirty as a police-station in London), a hook-nosed Saracen's Head with an immense quantity of black hair (there is a man attached to it) sells walking-sticks. On the other side of the doorway, a lady with a showy handkerchief for head-dress (wife to the Saracen's Head, I believe) sells articles of her own knitting; and sometimes flowers. A little further in, two or three blind men occasionally beg. Sometimes, they are visited by a man without legs, on a little go-cart, but who has such a fresh-coloured, lively face, and such a respectable, well-conditioned body, that he looks as if he had sunk into the ground up to his middle, or had come, but partially, up a flight of cellar-steps to speak to somebody. A little further in, a few men, perhaps, lie asleep in the middle of the day; or they may be chairmen waiting for their absent freight. If so, they have brought their chairs in with them, and there *they* stand also. On the left of the hall is a little room: a hatter's shop. On the first floor, is the English bank. On the first floor also, is a whole house, and a good large residence too. Heaven knows what there may be above that; but when you are there, you have only just begun to go upstairs. And yet, coming downstairs again, thinking of this; and passing out at a great crazy door in the back of the hall, instead of turning the other way, to get into the street again; it bangs behind you making the dismallest and most lonesome echoes, and you stand in a yard (the yard of the same house) which seems to have been unvisited by human foot, for a hundred years. Not a sound disturbs its repose. Not a head, thrust out of any of the grim, dark, jealous windows, within sight, makes the weeds in the cracked pavement faint of heart, by suggesting the possibility of there being hands to grub them up. Opposite to you, is a giant figure carved in stone, reclining, with an urn, upon a lofty piece of artificial rock-work; and out of the urn, dangles the fag end of a leaden pipe, which, once upon a time, poured a small torrent down the rocks. But the eye-sockets of the giant are not drier than this channel is now. He seems to have given his urn, which is nearly upside down, a final tilt; and after crying, like a sepulchral child, 'All gone!' to have lapsed into a stony silence.

In the streets of shops, the houses are much smaller, but of great size notwithstanding, and extremely high. They are very dirty: quite undrained, if my nose be at all reliable: and emit a peculiar fragrance, like the smell of very bad cheese, kept in very hot blankets. Notwithstanding the height of the houses, there would seem to have been a lack of room in the City, for new houses are thrust in everywhere, Wherever it has been possible to cram a tumble-down tenement into a crack or corner, in it has gone. If there be a nook or angle in the wall of a church, or a crevice in any other dead wall, of any sort, there you are sure to find some kind of habitation: looking as if it had grown there, like a fungus. Against the Government House, against the old Senate House, round about any large building, little shops stick so close, like parasite vermin to the great carcase. And for all this, look where you may: up steps, down steps, anywhere, everywhere: there are irregular houses, receding, starting forward, tumbling down, leaning against their neighbours, crippling themselves or their friends by some means or other, until one, more irregular than the rest, chokes up the way, and you can't see any further.

One of the rottenest-looking parts of the town, I think, is down by the landing-wharf: though it may be, that its being associated with a great deal of rottenness on the evening of our arrival, has stamped it deeper in my mind. Here, again, the houses are very high, and are of an infinite variety of deformed shapes, and have (as most of the houses have) something hanging out of a great many windows, and wafting its frowzy fragrance on the breeze. Sometimes, it is a curtain; sometimes, it is a carpet; sometimes, it is a bed; sometimes, a whole lineful of clothes; but there is almost always something. Before the basement of these houses, is an arcade over the pavement: very massive, dark, and low, like an old crypt. The stone, or plaster, of which it is made, has turned quite black; and against every one of these black piles, all sorts of filth and garbage seem to accumulate spontaneously. Beneath some of the arches, the sellers of maccaroni and polenta establish their stalls, which are by no means inviting. The offal of a fish-market, near at hand – that is to say, of a back lane, where people sit upon the ground and on various old bulkheads and sheds, and sell fish when they have any to dispose of – and of a vegetable market, constructed on the same principle – are contributed to the decoration of this quarter; and as all the mercantile business is transacted here, and it is crowded all day, it has a very decided flavour about it. The Porto Franco, or Free Port (where goods brought in from foreign countries pay no duty until they are sold and taken out, as in a bonded warehouse in England), is down here also; and two portentous officials, in cocked hats, stand at the gate to search you if they choose, and to keep out Monks and Ladies. For, Sanctity as well as Beauty has been known to yield to the temptation of smuggling, and in the same way: that is to say, by concealing the smuggled property beneath the loose folds of its dress. So Sanctity and Beauty may, by no means, enter.

The streets of Genoa would be all the better for the importation of a few Priests of prepossessing appearance. Every fourth or fifth man in the streets is a Priest or a Monk; and there is pretty sure to be at least one itinerant ecclesiastic inside or outside every hackney carriage on the neighbouring roads. I have no knowledge, elsewhere, of more repulsive countenances than are to be found among these gentry. If Nature's handwriting be at all legible, greater varieties of sloth, deceit, and intellectual torpor, could hardly be observed among any class of men in the world.

MR PEPYS once heard a clergyman assert in his sermon, in illustration of his respect for the Priestly office, that if he could meet a Priest and angel together, he would salute the Priest first. I am rather of the opinion of PETRARCH, who, when his pupil BOCCACCIO wrote to him in great tribulation, that he had been visited and admonished for his writings by a Carthusian Friar who claimed to be a messenger immediately commissioned by Heaven for that purpose, replied, that for his own part, he would take the liberty of testing the reality of the commission by personal observation of the Messenger's face, eyes, forehead, behaviour, and discourse. I cannot but believe myself, from similar observation, that many unaccredited celestial messengers may be seen skulking through the streets of Genoa, or droning away their lives in other Italian towns.

Perhaps the Cappuccini, though not a learned body, are, as an order, the best friends of the people. They seem to mingle with them more immediately, as their counsellors and comforters; and to go among them more, when they are sick; and to pry less than some other orders, into the secrets of families, for the purpose of establishing a baleful ascendency over their weaker members; and to be influenced by a less fierce desire to make converts, and once made, to let them go to ruin, soul and body. They may be seen, in their coarse dress, in all parts of the town at all times, and begging in the markets early in the morning. The Jesuits too, muster strong in the streets, and go slinking noiselessly about, in pairs, like black cats.

In some of the narrow passages, distinct trades congregate. There is a street of jewellers, and there is a row of booksellers; but even down in places where nobody ever can, or ever could, penetrate in a carriage, there are mighty old palaces shut in among the gloomiest and closest walls, and almost shut out from the sun. Very few of the tradesmen have any idea of setting forth their goods, or disposing them for show. If you, a stranger, want to buy anything, you usually look round the shop till you see it; then clutch it, if it be within reach, and inquire how much. Everything is sold at the most unlikely place. If you want coffee, you go to a sweetmeat shop; and if you want meat, you will probably find it behind an old checked curtain, down half-a-dozen steps, in some sequestered nook as hard to find as if the commodity were poison, and Genoa's law were death to any that uttered it.

Most of the apothecaries' shops are great lounging-places. Here, grave men with sticks, sit down in the shade for hours together, passing a meagre Genoa paper from hand to hand, and talking, drowsily and sparingly, about the News. Two or three of these are poor physicians, ready to proclaim themselves on an emergency, and tear off with any messenger who may arrive. You may know them by the way in which they stretch their necks to listen, when you enter; and by the sigh with which they fall back again into their dull corners, on finding that you only want medicine. Few people lounge in the barbers' shops; though they are very numerous, as hardly any man shaves himself. But the apothecary's has its group of loungers, who sit back among the bottles, with their hands folded over the tops of their sticks. So still and quiet, that either you don't see them in the darkened shop, or mistake them – as I did one ghostly man in bottle-green, one day, with a hat like a stopper – for Horse Medicine.

THE THEATRES

There are three theatres in the city, besides an old one now rarely opened. The most important – the Carlo Felice: the opera-house of Genoa – is a very splendid, commodious, and beautiful theatre. A company of comedians were acting there, when we arrived: and soon after their departure, a second-rate opera company came. The great season is not until the carnival time - in the spring. Nothing impressed me, so much, in my visits here (which were pretty numerous) as the uncommonly hard and cruel character of the audience, who resent the slightest defect, take nothing good-humouredly, seem to be always lying in wait for an opportunity to hiss, and spare the actresses as little as the actors. But, as there is nothing else of a public nature at which they are allowed to express the least disapprobation, perhaps they are resolved to make the most of this opportunity.

There are a great number of Piedmontese officers too, who are allowed the privilege of kicking their heels in the pit, for next to nothing: gratuitous, or cheap accommodation for these gentlemen being insisted on, by the Governor, in all public or semi-public entertainments. They are lofty critics in consequence, and infinitely more exacting than if they made the unhappy manager's fortune.

The Teatro Diurno, or Day Theatre, is a covered stage in the open air, where the performances take place by daylight, in the cool of the afternoon; commencing at four or five o'clock, and lasting some three hours. It is curious, sitting among the audience, to have a fine view of the neighbouring hills and houses, and to see the neighbours at their windows looking on, and to hear the bells of the churches and convents ringing at most complete cross-purposes with the scene. Beyond this, and the novelty of seeing a play in the fresh pleasant air, with the darkening evening closing in, there is nothing very exciting or characteristic in the performances. The actors are indifferent; and though they sometimes represent one of Goldoni's comedies, the staple of the Drama is French. Anything like nationality is dangerous to despotic governments, and Jesuit-beleaguered kings.

The Theatre of Puppets, or Marionetti – a famous company from Milan – is, without any exception, the drollest exhibition I ever beheld in my life. I never saw anything so exquisitely ridiculous. They *look* between four and five feet high, but are really much smaller; for when a musician in the orchestra happens to put his hat on the stage, it becomes alarmingly gigantic, and almost blots out an actor. They usually play a comedy, and a ballet. The comic man in the comedy I saw one summer night, is a waiter in an hotel. There never was such a locomotive actor, since the world began. Great pains are taken with him. He has extra joints in his legs: and a practical eye, with which he winks at the pit, in a manner that is absolutely insupportable to a stranger, but which the initiated audience, mainly composed of the common people, receive (so they do everything else) quite as a matter of course, and as if he were a man. His spirits are prodigious. He continually shakes his legs, and winks his eye. And there is a heavy father with grey hair, who sits down on the regular conventional stage-bank, and blesses his daughter in the regular conventional way, who is tremendous. No one would suppose it possible that anything short of a real man could be so tedious. It is the triumph of art.

In the ballet, an Enchanter runs away with the Bride, in the very hour of her nuptials. He brings her to his cave, and tries to soothe her. They sit down on a sofa (the regular sofa! in the regular place, O.P. Second Entrance!) and a procession of musicians enters; one creature playing a drum, and knocking himself off his legs at every blow. These failing to delight her, dancers appear. Four first; then two; *the* two; the flesh-coloured two. The way in which they dance; the height to which they spring;

the impossible and inhuman extent to which they pirouette; the revelation of their preposterous legs; the coming down with a pause, on the very tips of their toes, when the music requires it; the gentleman's retiring up, when it is the lady's turn; and the lady's retiring up, when it is the gentleman's turn; the final passion of a pas-de-deux; and the going off with a bound! – I shall never see a real ballet, with a composed countenance again.

THE PALAZZO PESCHIERE

There is not in Italy, they say (and I believe them), a lovelier residence than the Palazzo Peschiere, or Palace of the Fishponds, whither we removed as soon as our three months' tenancy of the Pink Jail at Albaro had ceased and determined.

It stands on a height within the walls of Genoa, but aloof from the town: surrounded by beautiful gardens of its own, adorned with statues, vases, fountains, marble basins, terraces, walks of orange-trees and lemon-trees, groves of roses and camellias. All its apartments are beautiful in their proportions and decorations; but the great hall, some fifty feet in height, with three large windows at the end, overlooking the whole town of Genoa, the harbour, and the neighbouring sea, affords one of the most fascinating and delightful prospects in the world. Any house more cheerful and habitable than the great rooms are, within, it would be difficult to conceive: and certainly nothing more delicious than the scene without, in sunshine or in moonlight, could be imagined. It is more like an enchanted place in an Eastern story than a grave and sober lodging.

How you may wander on, from room to room, and never tire of the wild fancies on the walls and ceilings, as bright in their fresh colouring as if they had been painted yesterday; or how one floor, or even the great hall which opens on eight other rooms, is a spacious promenade; or how there are corridors and bedchambers above, which we never use and rarely visit, and scarcely know the way through; or how there is a view of a perfectly different character on each of the four sides of the building; matters little. But that prospect from the hall is like a vision to me. I go back to it, in fancy, as I have done in calm reality a hundred times a day; and stand there, looking out, with the sweet scents from the garden rising up about me, in a perfect dream of happiness.

There lies all Genoa, in beautiful confusion, with its many churches, monasteries, and convents, pointing up into the sunny sky; and down below me, just where the roofs begin, a solitary convent parapet, fashioned like a gallery, with an iron across at the end, where sometimes early in the morning, I have seen a little group of dark-veiled nuns gliding sorrowfully to and fro, and stopping now and then to peep down upon the waking world in which they have no part. Old Monte Faccio, brightest of hills in good weather, but sulkiest when storms are coming on, is here, upon the left. The Fort within the walls (the good King built it to command the town, and beat the houses of the Genoese about their ears, in case they should be discontented) commands that height upon the right. The broad sea lies beyond, in front there; and that line of coast, beginning by the lighthouse, and tapering away, a mere speck in the rosy distance, is the beautiful coast road that leads to Nice. The garden near at hand, among the roofs and houses: all red with roses and fresh with little fountains: is the Acqua Sola – a public promenade, where the military band plays gaily, and the white veils cluster thick, and the Genoese nobility ride round, and round, and round, in state-clothes and coaches at least, if not in absolute wisdom. Within a stone's-throw, as it seems, the audience of the Day Theatre sit: their faces turned this way. But as the stage is hidden, it is very odd, without a knowledge of the cause, to see their faces changed so suddenly from earnestness to laughter; and odder still, to hear the rounds upon rounds of applause, rattling in the evening air, to which the curtain falls. But, being Sunday night, they act their best and most attractive play. And now, the sun is going down, in such magnificent array of red, and green, and golden light, as neither pen nor pencil could depict; and to the ringing of the vesper bells, darkness sets in at once, without a twilight. Then, lights begin to shine in Genoa, and on the country road; and the revolving lantern out at sea there, flashing, for an instant, on this palace front and portico, illuminates it as if there were a bright moon bursting from behind a cloud; then, merges it in deep obscurity. And this, so far as I know, is the only reason why the Genoese avoid it after dark, and think it haunted.

My memory will haunt it, many nights, in time to come; but nothing worse, I will engage. The same Ghost will occasionally sail away, as I did one pleasant autumn evening, into the bright prospect, and snuff the morning air at Marseilles.

No other period of his holidays in Europe has been so fully and freely described. But in my judgement Pictures from Italy *has always been strangely underestimated. It certainly is no mere guide-book, and the letters which he wrote at the same time are as arresting as the book itself. Who but Dickens would have responded with such zest and originality to the flow of Italian life, past and present, which surrounded him? And with his instinctive appreciation of the vagaries of everyday character, he could now present, perhaps with very little high-lighting, the people he saw in his daily perambulations and excursions in this foreign country.*

The ever-resourceful 'Brave' is often the centre of amusing, sometimes bizarre, situations, such as the episode when the pleasure-boat was detained in quarantine and he procured food for all the voyagers. In this story a very human but splendidly dignified Capuchin friar is also shown, in dramatic contrast with a fussy, conceited little Frenchman. This friar is notable for being one of the few admirable representatives of the Roman Catholic priesthood for whom Dickens came to have such understandable detestation, at that period (how different from our own!) only too well-founded.

THE COURIER, THE FRIAR AND THE FRENCHMAN

The steamer had come from Genoa in a delicious run of eighteen hours, and we were going to run back again by the Cornice road from Nice: not being satisfied to have seen only the outsides of the beautiful towns that rise in picturesque white clusters from among the olive woods, and rocks, and hills, upon the margin of the Sea.

The Boat which started for Nice that night, at eight o'clock, was very small, and so crowded with goods that there was scarcely room to move; neither was there anything to eat on board, except bread; nor to drink, except coffee. But being due at Nice at about eight or so in the morning, this was of no consequence: so when we began to wink at the bright stars, in involuntary acknowledgment of their winking at us, we turned into our berths, in a crowded, but cool little cabin, and slept soundly till morning.

The Boat, being as dull and dogged a little boat as ever was built, it was within an hour of noon when we turned into Nice Harbour, where we very little expected anything but breakfast. But we were laden with wool. Wool must not remain in the Custom-house at Marseilles more than twelve months at a stretch, without paying duty. It is the custom to make fictitious removals of unsold wool to evade this law; to take it somewhere when the twelve months are nearly out; bring it straight back again; and warehouse it, as a new cargo, for nearly twelve months longer. This wool of ours, had come originally from some place in the East. It was recognised as Eastern produce, the moment we entered the harbour. Accordingly, the gay little Sunday boats, full of holiday people, which had come off to greet us, were warned away by the authorities; we were declared in quarantine; and a great flag was solemnly run up to the mast-head on the wharf, to make it known to all the town.

It was a very hot day indeed. We were unshaved, unwashed, undressed, unfed, and could hardly enjoy the absurdity of lying blistering in a lazy harbour, with the town looking on from a respectful distance, all manner of whiskered men in cocked hats discussing our fate at a remote guard-house, with gestures (we looked very hard at them through telescopes) expressive of a week's detention at least: and nothing whatever the matter all the time. But even in this crisis the brave Courier achieved a triumph. He telegraphed somebody (*I* saw nobody) either naturally connected with the hotel, or put *en rapport* with the

Palazzo Peschiere, Genoa, where Dickens wrote *The Chimes*

establishment for that occasion only. The telegraph was answered, and in half an hour or less, there came a loud shout from the guard-house. The captain was wanted. Everybody helped the captain into his boat. Everybody got his luggage, and said we were going. The captain rowed away, and disappeared behind a little jutting corner of the Galley-slaves' Prison: and presently came back with something, very sulkily. The brave Courier met him at the side, and received the something as its rightful owner. It was a wicker basket, folded in a linen cloth; and in it were two great bottles of wine, a roast fowl, some salt fish chopped with garlic, a great loaf of bread, a dozen or so of peaches, and a few other trifles. When we had selected our own breakfast, the brave Courier invited a chosen party to partake of these refreshments, and assured them that they need not be deterred by motives of delicacy, as he would order a second basket to be furnished at their expense. Which he did – no one knew how – and by-and-by, the captain being again summoned, again sulkily returned with another something; over which my popular attendant presided as before: carving with a clasp-knife, his own personal property, something smaller than a Roman sword.

The whole party on board were made merry by these unexpected supplies; but none more so than a loquacious little Frenchman, who got drunk in five minutes, and a sturdy Cappuccíno Friar, who had taken everybody's fancy mightily, and was one of the best friars in the world, I verily believe.

He had a free, open countenance; and a rich brown, flowing beard; and was a remarkably handsome man, of about fifty. He had come up to us, early in the morning, and inquired whether we were sure to be at Nice by eleven; saying that he particularly wanted to know, because if we reached it by that time he would have to perform Mass, and must deal with the consecrated wafer, fasting; whereas, if there were no chance of his being in time, he would immediately breakfast. He made this communication, under the idea that the brave Courier was the captain; and indeed he looked much more like it than anybody else on board. Being assured that we should arrive in good time, he fasted, and talked, fasting, to everybody, with the most charming good humour; answering jokes at the expense of friars, with other jokes at the expense of laymen, and saying that, friar as he was, he would engage to take up the two strongest men on board, one after the other, with his teeth, and carry them along the deck. Nobody gave him the opportunity, but I dare say he could have done it; for he was a gallant, noble figure of a man, even in the Cappuccíno dress, which is the ugliest and most ungainly that can well be.

All this had given great delight to the loquacious Frenchman, who gradually patronised the Friar very much, and seemed to commiserate him as one who might have been born a Frenchman himself, but for an unfortunate destiny. Although his patronage was such as a mouse might bestow upon a lion, he had a vast opinion of its condescension; and in the warmth of that sentiment, occasionally rose on tiptoe, to slap the Friar on the back.

When the baskets arrived: it being then too late for Mass: the Friar went to work bravely: eating prodigiously of the cold meat and bread, drinking deep draughts of the wine, smoking cigars, taking snuff, sustaining an uninterrupted conversation with all hands, and occasionally running to the boat's side and hailing somebody on shore with the intelligence that we *must* be got out of this quarantine somehow or other, as he had to take part in a great religious procession in the afternoon. After this, he would come back, laughing lustily from pure good humour: while the Frenchman wrinkled his small face into ten thousand creases, and said how droll it was, and what a brave boy was that Friar! At length the heat of the sun without, and the wine within, made the Frenchman sleepy. So, in the noontide of his patronage of his gigantic protégé, he lay down among the wool, and began to snore.

It was four o'clock before we were released; and the Frenchman, dirty and woolly, and snuffy, was still sleeping when the Friar went ashore. As soon as we were free, we all hurried away, to wash and dress, that we might make a decent appearance at the procession; and I saw no more of the Frenchman until we took up our station in the main street to see it pass, when he squeezed himself into a front place, elaborately renovated; threw back his little coat, to show a broad-barred velvet waistcoat, sprinkled all over with stars; then adjusted himself and his cane so as utterly to bewilder and transfix the Friar, when he should appear.

The procession was a very long one, and included an immense number of people divided into small parties; each party chanting nasally, on its own account, without reference to any other, and producing a most dismal result. There were angels, crosses, Virgins carried on flat boards surrounded by Cupids, crowns, saints, missals, infantry, tapers, monks, nuns, relics, dignitaries of the church in green hats, walking under crimson parasols: and, here and there, a species of sacred street-lamp hoisted on a pole. We looked out anxiously for the Cappuccíni, and presently their brown robes and corded girdles were seen coming on, in a body.

I observed the little Frenchman chuckle over the idea that when the Friar saw him in the broad-barred waistcoat, he would mentally exclaim, 'Is that my Patron! *That* distinguished man!' and would be covered with confusion. Ah! never was the Frenchman so deceived. As our friend the Cappuccíno advanced, with folded arms, he looked straight into the visage of the little Frenchman, with a bland, serene, composed abstraction, not to be described. There was not the faintest trace of recognition or amusement on his features; not the smallest consciousness of bread and meat, wine, snuff, or cigars. 'C'est lui-même,' I heard the little Frenchman say, in some doubt. Oh yes, it was himself. It was not his brother or his nephew, very like him. It was he. He walked in great state; being one of the Superiors of the Order: and looked his part to admiration. There never was anything so perfect of its kind as the contemplative way in which he allowed his placid gaze to rest on us, his late companions, as if he had never seen us in his life and didn't see us then. The Frenchman, quite humbled, took off his hat at last, but the Friar still passed on, with the same imperturbable serenity; and the broad-barred waistcoat, fading into the crowd, was seen no more.

The Adventure of 'The Chimes'

Even while planning to enjoy an almost complete holiday, however, Dickens could not escape the corroding thoughts of the miseries of other people, not only in Italy but in his own country. It was now 'the hungry forties', when the poorest people were driven to attempt suicide, often to be hauled out of the Thames and savagely punished for trying to end their own and sometimes their children's miserable lives.

Dickens, having been elated by the success of his first Christmas book, A Christmas Carol, *decided to write another to celebrate Christmas 1844, and once more to arouse sympathy with the underdogs of society. So, burning with compassion, he sat down one day to begin writing. Then all the church bells in Genoa started ringing, a jangling cacophony. They went on and on, and he found it impossible to think of a title for his book; and it was one of his idiosyncrasies that he* must *always have his title before he could begin writing. The bells went on day after day and he thought they would drive him mad.*

But strangely enough it was they who gave him a sudden idea. Soon Forster received a cryptic but reassuring note: 'We have heard THE CHIMES at midnight, Master Shallow'.

He paid heavily for the writing of The Chimes. *'It has great possession of me night and day and drags me where it will . . . My cheeks, which were beginning to fill out, have sunk again; my eyes have grown immensely large: and the head inside the hair is hot and giddy. Read the scene at the end of the third part twice. I wouldn't write it twice for something.'*

The book had engaged him so vitally that he felt an irresistible impulse to go to London before Christmas and read it to a select company of friends in Forster's room in Lincoln's Inn. So, in the face of every argument against such a wild-cat scheme, involving, of course, hazards and delays unheard-of today, he set out on 6 November with the faithful Roche to travel, first on a sight-seeing elliptical journey through Northern Italy, and thence, via Switzerland, Germany and France, to London.

By means of a variety of erratic coaches, one of which was 'as small as a fly' and another 'like a travelling caravan', they visited Piacenza, Parma, Stradella, Modena, Bologna, Ferrara and Venice. Thence, turning about, they came westwards by Verona and Mantua to Milan. Here they stayed for two days with Kate and Georgina who had come up from Genoa to meet them, bringing their mail. Then Dickens and Roche resumed their journey via the Simplon Pass, Geneva, Fribourg and Strasbourg, and at last, after fifty hours travelling by diligence in bitter weather, they reached Paris. And so to London, where, on 31 November, he was rapturously greeted by Forster and Maclise.

Pictures from Italy *gives characteristic impressions of all this journeying and exploring. Side by side with the ups-and-downs, absurdities, inconveniences and small pleasures which he describes with his usual gusto, there are times when, 'in a strange, half-sorrowful, half-delicious doze', he wanders about in places such as Piacenza whose very dullness – indeed, the duller they are the better – is a quaint, unexpected sort of inspiration. In these pages too we have glimpses of his gentle tact in dealing with poor humble men, such as the little cicerone in Mantua, whom he 'would as soon have trodden on as dismissed' when he came peering in at the half-open door to offer his services.*

FROM PARMA TO MANTUA

Parma has cheerful, stirring streets, for an Italian town; and consequently is not so characteristic as many places of less note. Always excepting the retired Piazza, where the Cathedral, Baptistery, and Campanile – ancient buildings, of a sombre brown, embellished with innumerable grotesque monsters and dreamy-looking creatures carved in marble and red stone – are clustered in a noble and magnificent repose. Their silent presence was only invaded, when I saw them, by the twittering of the many birds that were flying in and out of the crevices in the stones and little nooks in the architecture, where they had made their nests. They were busy, rising from the cold shade of Temples made with hands, into the sunny air of Heaven. Not so the worshippers within, who were listening to the same drowsy chaunt, or kneeling before the same kinds of images and tapers, or whispering, with their heads bowed down, in the selfsame dark confessionals, as I had left in Genoa and everywhere else.

The decayed and mutilated paintings with which this church is covered, have, to my thinking, a remarkably mournful and depressing influence. It is miserable to see great works of art – something of the Souls of Painters – perishing and fading away, like human forms. This cathedral is odorous with the rotting of Correggio's frescoes in the Cupola. Heaven knows how beautiful they may have been at one time. Connoisseurs fall into raptures with them now; but such a labyrinth of arms and legs: such heaps of foreshortened limbs, entangled and involved and jumbled together: no operative surgeon, gone mad, could imagine in his wildest delirium.

There is a very interesting subterranean church here: the roof supported by marble pillars, behind each of which there seemed to be at least one beggar in ambush: to say nothing of the tombs and secluded altars. From every one of these lurking-places, such crowds of phantom-looking men and women, leading other men and women with twisted limbs, or chattering jaws, or paralytic gestures, or idiotic heads, or some other sad infirmity, came hobbling out to beg, that if the ruined frescoes in the cathedral above, had been suddenly animated, and had retired to this lower church, they could hardly have made a greater confusion, or exhibited a more confounding display of arms and legs.

There is Petrarch's Monument, too; and there is the Baptistery, with its beautiful arches and immense font; and there is a gallery containing some very remarkable pictures, whereof a few were being copied by hairy-faced artists, with little velvet caps more off their heads than on. There is the Farnese Palace, too; and in it one of the dreariest spectacles of decay that ever was seen – a grand, old, gloomy theatre, mouldering away.

It is a large wooden structure, of the horse-shoe shape; the lower seats arranged upon the Roman plan, but above them, great heavy chambers, rather than boxes, where the Nobles sat, remote in their proud state. Such desolation as has fallen on this theatre, enhanced in the spectator's fancy by its gay intention and design, none but worms can be familiar with. A hundred and ten years have passed, since any play was acted here. The sky shines in through the gashes in the roof; the boxes are dropping down, wasting away, and only tenanted by rats; damp and mildew smear the faded colours, and make spectral maps upon the panels; lean rags are dangling down where there were gay festoons on the Proscenium; the stage has rotted so, that a narrow wooden gallery is thrown across it, or it would sink beneath the tread, and bury the visitor in the gloomy depth beneath. The desolation and decay impress themselves on all the senses. The air has a mouldering smell, and an earthy taste; any stray outer sounds that straggle in with some lost sunbeam, are muffled and heavy; and the worm, the maggot, and the rot have changed the surface of the wood beneath the touch, as time will seam and roughen a smooth hand. If ever Ghosts act plays, they act them on this ghostly stage.

It was most delicious weather, when we came into Modena, where the darkness of the sombre colonnades over the footways skirting the main street on either side, was made refreshing and agreeable by the bright sky, so wonderfully blue. I passed from all the glory of the day, into a dim cathedral, where High Mass was performing, feeble tapers were burning, people were kneeling in all directions before all manner of shrines, and officiating priests were crooning the usual chant, in the usual, low, dull, drawling, melancholy tone.

Thinking how strange it was, to find, in every stagnant town, this same Heart beating with the same monotonous pulsation, the centre of the same torpid, listless system, I came out by another door, and was suddenly scared to death by a blast from the shrillest trumpet that ever was blown. Immediately, came tearing round the corner, an equestrian company from Paris: marshalling themselves under the walls of the church, and flouting, with their horses' heels, the griffins, lions, tigers, and other monsters in stone and marble, decorating its exterior. First, there came a stately nobleman with a great deal of hair, and no hat, bearing an enormous banner, on which was inscribed, MAZEPPA! TONIGHT! Then, a Mexican chief, with a great pear-shaped club on his shoulder, like Hercules. Then, six or eight Roman chariots: each with a beautiful lady in extremely short petticoats, and unnaturally pink tights, erect within: shedding beaming looks upon the crowd, in which there was a latent expression of discomposure and anxiety, for which I couldn't account, until, as the open back of each chariot presented itself, I saw the immense difficulty with which the pink legs maintained their perpendicular, over the uneven pavement of the town: which gave me quite a new idea of the ancient Romans and Britons. The procession was brought to a close, by some dozen indomitable warriors of different nations, riding two and two, and haughtily surveying the tame population of Modena: among whom, however, they occasionally condescended to scatter largesse in the form of a few handbills. After caracolling among the lions and tigers, and proclaiming that evening's entertainments with blast of trumpet, it then filed off, by the other end of the square, and left a new and greatly increased dulness behind.

When the procession had so entirely passed away, that the shrill trumpet was mild in the distance, and the tail of the last horse was hopelessly round the corner, the people who had come out of the church to stare at it, went back again. But one old lady, kneeling on the pavement within, near the door, had seen it all, and had been immensely interested, without getting up; and this old lady's eye, at that juncture, I happened to catch: to our mutual confusion. She cut our embarrassment very short, however, by crossing herself devoutly, and going down, at full length, on her face, before a figure in a fancy petticoat and a gilt crown; which was so like one of the procession-figures, that perhaps at this hour she may think the whole appearance a celestial vision. Anyhow, I must certainly have forgiven her her interest in the Circus, though I had been her Father Confessor.

There was a little fiery-eyed old man with a crooked shoulder, in the cathedral, who took it very ill that I made no effort to see the bucket (kept in an old tower) which the people of Modena took away from the people of Bologna in the fourteenth century, and about which there was war made and a mock-heroic poem by TASSONE, too. Being quite content, however, to look at the outside of the tower, and feast, in imagination, on the bucket within; and preferring to loiter in the shade of the tall Campanile, and about the cathedral; I have no personal knowledge of this bucket, even at the present time.

Indeed, we were at Bologna, before the little old man (or the Guide-Book) would have considered that we had half done justice to the wonders of Modena. But it is such a delight to me to leave new scenes behind, and still go on, encountering newer scenes – and, moreover, I have such a perverse disposition in respect of sights that are cut, and dried, and dictated – that I fear I sin against similar authorities in every place I visit.

Be this as it may, in the pleasant Cemetery at Bologna, I found myself walking next Sunday morning, among the stately marble tombs and colonnades, in company with a crowd of Peasants, and escorted by a little Cicerone of that town, who was excessively anxious for the honour of the place, and most solicitous to divert my attention from the bad monuments: whereas he was never tired of extolling the good ones. Seeing this little man (a good-humoured little man he was, who seemed to have nothing in his face but shining teeth and eyes) looking wistfully at a certain plot of grass, I asked him who was buried there. 'The poor people, Signore,' he said, with a shrug and a smile, and stopping to look back at me – for he always went on a little before, and took off his hat to introduce every new monument. 'Only the poor, Signore! It's very cheerful. It's very lively. How green it is, how cool! It's like a meadow! There are five,' – holding up all the fingers of his right hand to express the number, which an Italian peasant will always do, if it be within the compass of his ten fingers, – 'there are five of my little children buried there, Signore; just there; a little to the right. Well! Thanks to God! It's very cheerful. How green it is, how cool it is! It's quite a meadow!'

He looked me very hard in the face, and seeing I was sorry for him, took a pinch of snuff (every Cicerone takes snuff), and made a little bow; partly in deprecation of his having alluded to such a subject, and partly in memory of the children and of his favourite saint. It was as unaffected and as perfectly natural a little bow, as ever man made. Immediately afterwards, he took his hat off altogether, and begged to introduce me to the next monument; and his eyes and his teeth shone brighter than before.

There was such a very smart official in attendance at the Cemetery where the little Cicerone had buried his children, that when the little Cicerone suggested to me, in a whisper, that there would be no offence in presenting this officer, in return for some slight extra service, with a couple of pauls (about tenpence, English money), I looked incredulously at his cocked hat, wash-leather gloves, well-made uniform, and dazzling buttons, and rebuked the little Cicerone with a grave shake of the head. For, in splendour of appearance, he was at least equal to the Deputy Usher of the Black Rod; and the idea of his carrying, as Jeremy Diddler would say, 'such a thing as tenpence' away with him, seemed monstrous. He took it in excellent part, however, when I made bold to give it him, and pulled off his cocked hat with a flourish that would have been a bargain at double the money.

It seemed to be his duty to describe the monuments to the people – at all events he was doing so; and when I compared him, like Gulliver in Brobdingnag, 'with the Institutions of my own beloved country, I could not refrain from tears of pride and exultation.' He had no pace at all; no more than a tortoise. He loitered as the people loitered, that they might gratify their curiosity; and positively allowed them, now and then, to read the inscriptions on the tombs. He was neither shabby, nor insolent, nor churlish, nor ignorant. He spoke his own language with perfect propriety, and seemed to consider himself, in his way, a kind of teacher of the people, and to entertain a just respect both for himself and them. They would no more have such a man for a Verger in Westminster Abbey, than they would let the people in (as they do at Bologna) to see the monuments for nothing.

[In Mantua] I put up at the Hotel of the Golden Lion, and was in my own room arranging plans with the brave Courier, when there came a modest little tap at the door, which opened on an outer gallery surrounding a court-yard; and an intensely shabby little man looked in, to inquire if the gentleman would have a Cicerone to show the town. His face was so very wistful and anxious, in the half-opened doorway, and there was so much poverty expressed in his faded suit and little pinched hat, and in the threadbare worsted glove with which he held it – not expressed the less, because these were evidently his genteel clothes, hastily slipped on – that I would as soon have trodden on him as dismissed him. I engaged him on the instant, and he stepped in directly.

While I finished the discussion in which I was engaged, he stood, beaming by himself in a corner, making a feint of brushing my hat with his arm. If his fee had been as many napoleons as it was francs, there could not have shot over the twilight of his shabbiness such a gleam of sun, as lighted up the whole man, now that he was hired.

'Well!' said I, when I was ready, 'shall we go out now?'

'If the gentleman pleases. It is a beautiful day. A little fresh, but charming; altogether charming. The gentleman will allow me to open the door. This is the Inn Yard. The court-yard of the Golden Lion! The gentleman will please to mind his footing on the stairs.'

We were now in the street.

'This is the street of the Golden Lion. This, the outside of the Golden Lion. The interesting window up there, on the first *piano*, where the pane of glass is broken, is the window of the gentleman's chamber!'

Having viewed all these remarkable objects, I inquired if there were much to see in Mantua.

'Well! Truly, no. Not much! So, so,' he said, shrugging his shoulders apologetically.

'Many churches?'

'No. Nearly all suppressed by the French.'

'Monasteries or convents?'

'No. The French again! Nearly all suppressed by Napoleon.'

'Much business?'

'Very little business.'

'Many strangers?'

'Ah Heaven!'

I thought he would have fainted.

'Then, when we have seen the two large churches yonder, what shall we do next?' said I.

He looked up the street, and down the street, and rubbed his chin timidly; and then said, glancing in my face as if a light had broken on his mind, yet with a humble appeal to my forbearance that was perfectly irresistible:

'We can take a little turn about the town, Signore!' (Si può far' un piccolo giro della città).

It was impossible to be anything but delighted with the proposal, so we set off together in great good-humour. In the relief of his mind, he opened his heart, and gave up as much of Mantua as a Cicerone could.

'One must eat,' he said; 'but, bah! it was a dull place, without doubt!'

He made as much as possible of the Basilica of Santa Andrea – a noble church – and of an inclosed portion of the pavement, about which tapers were burning, and a few people kneeling, and under which is said to be preserved the Sangreal of the old Romances. This church disposed of, and another after it (the cathedral of San Pietro), we went to the Museum, which was shut up. 'It was all the same,' he said, 'Bah! There was not much inside!' Then, we went to see the Piazza del Diavolo, built by the Devil (for no particular purpose) in a single night; then, the Piazza Virgiliana; then, the statue of Virgil – *our* Poet, my little friend said, plucking up a spirit, for the moment, and putting his hat a little on one side. Then, we went to a dismal sort of farm-yard, by which a picture-gallery was approached. The moment the gate of this retreat was opened, some five hundred geese came waddling round us, stretching out their necks, and clamouring in the most hideous manner, as if they were ejaculating, 'Oh! here's somebody come to see the Pictures! Don't go up! Don't go up!' While we went up, they waited very quietly about the door in a crowd, cackling to one another occasionally, in a subdued tone; but the instant we appeared again, their necks came out like telescopes, and setting up a great noise, which meant, I have no doubt, 'What, you would go, would you? What do you think of it? How do you like it?' they attended us to the outer gate, and cast us forth, derisively, into Mantua.

The geese who saved the Capitol, were, as compared to these, Pork to the learned Pig. What a gallery it was! I would take their opinion on a question of art, in preference to the discourses of Sir Joshua Reynolds.

The never-to-be-forgotten climax, both geographically and spiritually, of this journey from Genoa to Milan was the city of Venice, 'the only thing', he wrote, 'I have ever been afraid to describe'. The only way in which he could suggest that impression of the mingled splendour, beauty and barbarity in which the city was so mysteriously enshrouded, was to imagine that he was dreaming rather than actually living through his whole fantastic experience there. That is why the chapter called 'An Italian Dream' is so different from any other.

AN ITALIAN DREAM

I had been travelling, for some days; resting very little in the night, and never in the day. The rapid and unbroken succession of novelties that had passed before me, came back like half-formed dreams; and a crowd of objects wandered in the greatest confusion through my mind, as I travelled on, by a solitary road. At intervals, some one among them would stop, as it were, in its restless flitting to and fro, and enable me to look at it, quite steadily, and behold it in full distinctness. After a few moments, it would dissolve, like a view in a magic-lantern; and while I saw some part of it quite plainly, and some faintly, and some not at all, would show me another of the many places I had lately seen, lingering behind it, and coming through it. This was no sooner visible than, in its turn, it melted into something else.

At one moment, I was standing again, before the brown old rugged churches of Modena. As I recognised the curious pillars with grim monsters for their bases, I seemed to see them, standing by themselves in the quiet square at Padua, where there were the staid old University, and the figures, demurely gowned, grouped here and there in the open space about it. Then, I was strolling in the outskirts of that pleasant city, admiring the unusual neatness of the dwelling-houses, gardens, and orchards, as I had seen them a few hours before. In their stead arose, immediately, the two towers of Bologna; and the most obstinate of all these objects, failed to hold its ground, a minute, before the monstrous moated castle of Ferrara, which, like an illustration to a wild romance, came back again in the red sunrise, lording it over the solitary, grass-grown, withered town. In short, I had that incoherent but delightful jumble in my brain, which travellers are apt to have, and are indolently willing to encourage. Every shake of the coach in which I sat, half dozing in the dark, appeared to jerk some new recollection out of its place, and to jerk some other new recollection into it; and in this state I fell asleep.

I was awakened after some time (as I thought) by the stopping of the coach. It was now quite night, and we were at the water-side. There lay here, a black boat, with a little house or cabin in it of the same mournful colour. When I had taken my seat in this, the boat was paddled, by two men, towards a great light, lying in the distance on the sea.

Ever and again, there was a dismal sigh of wind. It ruffled the water, and rocked the boat, and sent the dark clouds flying before the stars. I could not but think how strange it was, to be floating away at that hour: leaving the land behind, and going on, towards this light upon the sea. It soon began to burn brighter; and from being one light became a cluster of tapers, twinkling and shining out of the water, as the boat approached towards them by a dreamy kind of track, marked out upon the sea by posts and piles.

We had floated on, five miles or so, over the dark water, when I heard it rippling in my dream, against some obstruction near at hand. Looking out attentively, I saw, through the gloom, a something black and massive – like a shore, but lying close and flat upon the water, like a raft – which we were gliding past. The chief of the two rowers said it was a burial-place.

Full of the interest and wonder which a cemetery lying out there, in the lonely sea, inspired, I turned to gaze upon it as it should recede in our path, when it was quickly shut out from my view. Before I knew by what, or how, I found that we were gliding up a street – a phantom street; the houses rising on both sides, from the water, and the black boat gliding on beneath their windows. Lights were shining from some of these casements, plumbing the depth of the black stream with their reflected rays, but all was profoundly silent.

So we advanced into this ghostly city, continuing to hold our course through narrow streets and lanes, all filled and flowing with water. Some of the corners where our way branched off, were so acute and narrow, that it seemed impossible for the long slender boat to turn them; but the rowers, with a low melodious cry of warning, sent it skimming on without a pause. Sometimes, the rowers of another black boat like our own, echoed the cry, and slackening their speed (as I thought we did ours) would come flitting past us like a dark shadow. Other boats, of the same sombre hue, were lying moored, I thought, to painted pillars, near to dark mysterious doors that opened straight upon the water. Some of these were empty; in some, the rowers lay asleep; towards one, I saw some figures coming down a gloomy archway from the interior of a palace: gaily dressed, and attended by torch-bearers. It was but a glimpse I had of them; for a bridge, so low and close upon the boat that it seemed ready to fall down and crush us: one of the many bridges that perplexed the Dream: blotted them out, instantly. On we went, floating towards the heart of this strange place – with water all about us where never water was elsewhere – clusters of houses, churches, heaps of stately buildings growing out of it – and, everywhere, the same extraordinary silence. Presently, we shot across a broad and open stream; and passing, as I thought, before a spacious paved quay, where the bright lamps with which it was illuminated showed long rows of arches and pillars, of ponderous construction and great strength, but as light to the eye as garlands of hoar-frost or gossamer – and where, for the first time, I saw people walking – arrived at a flight of steps leading from the water to a large mansion, where, having passed through corridors and galleries innumerable, I lay down to rest; listening to the black boats stealing up and down the window on the rippling water, till I fell asleep.

The glory of the day that broke upon me in this Dream; its freshness, motion, buoyancy; its sparkles of the sun in water; its clear blue sky and rustling air; no waking words can tell. But, from my window, I looked down on boats and barks; on masts, sails, cordage, flags; on groups of busy sailors, working at the cargoes of these vessels; on wide quays, strewn with bales, casks, merchandise of many kinds; on great ships, lying near at hand in stately indolence; on islands, crowned with gorgeous domes and turrets: and where golden crosses glittered in the light, atop of wondrous churches, springing from the sea! Going down upon the margin of the green sea, rolling on before the door, and filling all the streets, I came upon a place of such surpassing beauty, and such grandeur, that all the rest was poor and faded, in comparison with its absorbing loveliness.

It was a great Piazza, as I thought; anchored, like all the rest, in the deep ocean. On its broad bosom, was a Palace, more majestic and magnificent in its old age, than all the buildings of the earth, in the high prime and fulness of their youth. Cloisters and galleries: so light, they might have been the work of fairy hands: so strong that centuries had battered them in vain: wound round and round this palace, and enfolded it with a Cathedral, gorgeous in the wild luxuriant fancies of the East. At no great distance from its porch, a lofty tower, standing by itself, and rearing its proud head, alone, into the sky, looked out upon the Adriatic Sea. Near to the margin of the stream, were two ill-omened pillars of red granite; one having on its top, a figure with a sword and shield; the other, a winged lion. Not

Dickens reading *The Chimes* to his friends, 2 December 1844

far from these again, a second tower: richest of the rich in all its decorations: even here, where all was rich: sustained aloft, a great orb, gleaming with gold and deepest blue: the Twelve Signs painted on it, and a mimic sun revolving in its course around them: while above, two bronze giants hammered out the hours upon a sounding bell. An oblong square of lofty houses of the whitest stone, surrounded by a light and beautiful arcade, formed part of this enchanted scene; and, here and there, gay masts for flags rose, tapering, from the pavement of the unsubstantial ground.

I thought I entered the Cathedral, and went in and out among its many arches: traversing its whole extent. A grand and dreamy structure, of immense proportions; golden with old mosaics; redolent of perfumes; dim with the smoke of incense; costly in treasure of precious stones and metals, glittering through iron bars; holy with the bodies of deceased saints; rainbow-hued with windows of stained glass; dark with carved woods and coloured marbles; obscure in its vast heights, and lengthened distances; shining with silver lamps and winking lights; unreal, fantastic, solemn, inconceivable throughout. I thought I entered the old palace; pacing silent galleries and council-chambers, where the old rulers of this mistress of the waters looked sternly out, in pictures, from the walls, and where her high-prowed galleys, still victorious on canvas, fought and conquered as of old. I thought I wandered through its halls of state and triumph – bare and empty now! – and musing on its pride and might, extinct: for that was past; all past: heard a voice say, 'Some tokens of its ancient rule and some consoling reasons for its downfall, may be traced here, yet!'

I dreamed that I was led on, then, into some jealous rooms, communicating with a prison near the palace; separated from it by a lofty bridge crossing a narrow street; and called, I dreamed, The Bridge of Sighs.

But first I passed two jagged slits in a stone wall; the lions' mouths – now toothless – where, in the distempered horror of my sleep, I thought denunciations of innocent men to the old wicked Council, had been dropped through, many a time, when the night was dark. So, when I saw the council-room to which such prisoners were taken for examination, and the door by which they passed out, when they were condemned – a door that never closed upon a man with life and hope before him – my heart appeared to die within me.

It was smitten harder though, when, torch in hand, I descended from the cheerful day into two ranges, one below another, of dismal, awful, horrible stone cells. They were quite dark. Each had a loop-hole in its massive wall, where, in the old time, every day, a torch was placed – I dreamed – to light the prisoner within, for half an hour. The captives, by the glimmering of these brief rays, had scratched and cut inscriptions in the blackened vaults. I saw them. For their labour with a rusty nail's point, had outlived their agony and them, through many generations.

One cell, I saw, in which no man remained for more than four-and-twenty hours; being marked for dead before he entered it. Hard by, another, and a dismal one, whereto, at midnight, the confessor came – a monk brown-robed, and hooded – ghastly in the day, and free bright air, but in the midnight of that murky prison, Hope's extinguisher, and Murder's herald. I had my foot upon the spot, where, at the same dread hour, the shriven prisoner was strangled; and struck my hand upon the guilty door – low-browed and stealthy – through which the lumpish sack was carried out into a boat, and rowed away, and drowned where it was death to cast a net.

Around this dungeon stronghold, and above some part of it: licking the rough walls without, and smearing them with damp and slime within: stuffing dank weeds and refuse into chinks and crevices, as if the very stones and bars had mouths to stop: furnishing a smooth road for the removal of the bodies of the secret victims of the State – a road so ready that it went along with them, and ran before them, like a cruel officer – flowed the same water that filled this Dream of mine, and made it seem one, even at the time.

Descending from the palace by a staircase, called, I thought, the Giant's – I had some imaginary recollection of an old man abdicating, coming, more slowly and more feebly, down it, when he heard the bell, proclaiming his successor – I glided off, in one of the dark boats, until we came to an old arsenal guarded by four marble lions. To make my Dream more monstrous and unlikely, one of these had words and sentences upon its body, inscribed there, at an unknown time, and in an unknown language; so that their purport was a mystery to all men.

There was little sound of hammers in this place for building ships, and little work in progress; for the greatness of the city was no more, as I have said. Indeed, it seemed a very wreck found drifting on the sea; a strange flag hoisted in its honourable stations, and strangers standing at its helm. A splendid barge in which its ancient chief had gone forth, pompously, at certain periods, to wed the ocean, lay here, I thought, no more; but, in its place, there was a tiny model, made from recollection like the city's greatness; and it told of what had been (so are the strong and weak confounded in the dust) almost as eloquently as the massive pillars, arches, roofs, reared to overshadow stately ships that had no other shadow now, upon the water or the earth.

An armoury was there yet. Plundered and despoiled; but an armoury. With a fierce standard taken from the Turks, drooping in the dull air of its cage. Rich suits of mail worn by great warriors were hoarded there; crossbows and bolts; quivers full of arrows; spears; swords, daggers, maces, shields, and heavy-headed axes. Plates of wrought steel and iron, to make the gallant horse a monster cased in metal scales; and one spring-weapon (easy to be carried in the breast) designed to do its office noiselessly, and made for shooting men with poisoned darts.

One press or case I saw, full of accursed instruments of torture: horribly contrived to cramp, and pinch, and grind and crush men's bones, and tear and twist them with the torment of a thousand deaths. Before it, were two iron helmets, with breast-pieces: made to close up tight and smooth upon the heads of living sufferers; and fastened on to each, was a small knob or anvil, where the directing devil could repose his elbow at his ease, and listen, near the walled-up ear, to the lamentations and confessions of the wretch within. There was that grim resemblance in them to the human shape – they were such moulds of sweating faces, pained and cramped – that it was difficult to think them empty; and terrible distortions lingering within them, seemed to follow me, when, taking to my boat again, I rowed off to a kind of garden or public walk in the sea, where there were grass and trees. But I forgot them when I stood upon its farthest brink – I stood there, in my dream – and looked, along the ripple, to the setting sun; before me, in the sky and on the deep, a crimson flush; and behind me the whole city resolving into streaks of red and purple, on the water.

In the luxurious wonder of so rare a dream, I took but little heed of time, and had but little understanding of its flight. But there were days and nights in it; and when the sun was high, and when the rays of lamps were crooked in the running water, I was still afloat, I thought: plashing the slippery walls and houses with the cleavings of the tide, as my black boat, borne upon it, skimmed along the streets.

Sometimes, alighting at the doors of churches and vast palaces, I wandered on, from room to room, from aisle to aisle, through labyrinths of rich altars, ancient monuments; decayed apartments where the furniture, half awful, half grotesque, was mouldering away. Pictures were there, replete with such enduring beauty and expression: with such passion, truth and power: that they seemed so many young and fresh realities among a host of spectres. I thought these, often intermingled with the old days of the city: with its beauties, tyrants, captains, patriots, merchants, courtiers, priests: nay, with its very stones, and bricks, and public places; all of which lived again, about me, on the walls. Then, coming down some marble staircase where the water lapped and oozed against the lower steps, I passed into my boat again, and went on in my dream.

Floating down narrow lanes, where carpenters, at work with plane and chisel in their shops, tossed the light shaving straight upon the water, where it lay like weed, or ebbed away before me in a tangled heap. Past open doors, decayed and rotten from long steeping in the wet, through which some scanty patch of vine shone green and bright, making unusual shadows on the pavement with its trembling leaves. Past quays and terraces, where women, gracefully veiled, were passing and repassing, and where idlers were reclining in the sunshine, on flat-stones and on flights of steps. Past bridges, where there were idlers too; loitering and looking over. Below stone balconies, erected at a giddy height, before the loftiest windows of the loftiest houses. Past plots of garden, theatres, shrines, prodigious piles of architecture – Gothic – Saracenic – fanciful with all the fancies of all times and countries. Past buildings that were high, and low, and black, and white, and straight, and crooked; mean and grand, crazy and strong. Twining among a tangled lot of boats and barges, and shooting out at last into a Grand Canal! There, in the errant fancy of my dream, I saw old Shylock passing to and fro upon a bridge, all built upon with shops and humming with the tongues of men; a form I seemed to know for Desdemona's, leaned down through a latticed blind to pluck a flower. And, in the dream, I thought that Shakespeare's spirit was abroad upon the water somewhere: stealing through the city.

At night, when two votive lamps burnt before an image of the Virgin, in a gallery outside the great cathedral, near the roof, I fancied that the great piazza of the Winged Lion was a blaze of cheerful light, and that its whole arcade was thronged with people; while crowds were diverting themselves in splendid coffee-houses opening from it – which were never shut, I thought, but open all night long. When the bronze giants struck the hour of midnight on the bell, I thought the life and animation of the city were all centred here; and as I rowed away, abreast the silent quays, I only saw them dotted, here and there, with sleeping boatmen wrapped up in their cloaks, and lying at full length upon the stones.

But close about the quays and churches, palaces and prisons: sucking at their walls, and welling up into the secret places of the town: crept the water always. Noiseless and watchful: coiled round and round it, in its many folds, like an old serpent: waiting for the time, I thought, when people should look down into its depths for any stone of the old city that had claimed to be its mistress.

Thus it floated me away, until I awoke in the old market-place at Verona. I have, many and many a time, thought since, of this strange Dream upon the water: half-wondering if it lie there yet, and if its name be VENICE.

But from Lodi he sent Forster news of the more everyday side of his travels – of the inn – and some intriguing glimpses of that highly original courier Roche.

NEWS FROM LODI

It is a great thing – quite a matter of course – with English travellers, to decry the Italian inns. Of course you have no comforts that you are used to in England; and travelling alone, you dine in your bedroom always: which is opposed to our habits. But they are immeasurably better than you would suppose. The attendants are very quick; very punctual; and so obliging, if you speak to them politely, that you would be a beast not to look cheerful, and take everything pleasantly. I am writing this in a room like a room on the two-pair front of an unfinished house in Eaton Square: the very walls make me feel as if I were a bricklayer distinguished by Mr Cubitt with the favour of having it to take care of. The windows won't open, and the doors won't shut; and these latter (a cat could get in, between them and the floor) have a windy command of a colonnade which is open to the night, so that my slippers positively blow off my feet, and make little circuits in the room – like leaves. There is a very ashy wood-fire, burning on an immense hearth which has no fender (there is no such thing in Italy); and it only knows two extremes – an agony of heat when wood is put on, and an agony of cold when it has been on two minutes. There is also an uncomfortable stain in the wall, where the fifth door (not being strictly indispensable) was walled up a year or two ago, and never painted over. But the bed is clean; and I have had an excellent dinner; and without being obsequious or servile, which is not at all the characteristic of the people in the north of Italy, the waiters are so amiably disposed to invent little attentions which they suppose to be English, and are so lighthearted and good-natured, that it is a pleasure to have to do with them. But so it is with all the people. *Vetturino*-travelling involves a stoppage of two hours in the middle of the day to bait the horses. At that time I always walk on. If there are many turns in the road, I necessarily have to ask my way, very often; and the men are such gentlemen, and the women such ladies, that it is quite an interchange of courtesies.

The brave C. continues to be a prodigy. He puts out my clothes at every inn as if I were going to stay there twelve months; calls me to the instant every morning; lights the fire before I get up; gets hold of roast fowls and produces them in coaches at a distance from all other help, in hungry moments; and is invaluable to me. He is such a good fellow, too, that little rewards don't spoil him. I always give him, after I have dined, a tumbler of Sauterne or Hermitage or whatever I may have; sometimes (as yesterday) when we have come to a public-house at about eleven o'clock, very cold, having started before day-break and had nothing. I make him take his breakfast with me; and this renders him only more anxious than ever, by redoubling attentions, to show me that he thinks he has got a good master. . . . I didn't tell you that the day before I left Genoa, we had a dinner-party – our English consul and his wife; the banker; Sir George Crawford and his wife; the De la Rues; Mr Curry; and some others, fourteen in all. At about nine in the morning, two men in immense paper caps inquired at the door for the brave C., who presently introduced them in triumph as the governor's cooks, his private friends, who had come to dress the dinner! Jane wouldn't stand this, however; so we were obliged to decline. Then there came, at half-hourly intervals, six gentlemen having the appearance of English clergymen, being other private friends who had come to wait. . . . We accepted *their* services; and you never saw anything so nicely and quietly done. He had asked, as a special distinction, to be allowed the supreme control of the dessert; and he had ices made like fruit, had pieces of crockery turned upside-down so as to look like other pieces of crockery non-existent in this part of Europe, and carried a case of toothpicks in his pocket. Then his delight was, to get behind Kate at one end of the table, to look at me at the other, and to say to Georgy in a low voice whenever he handed her anything, 'What does master think of datter 'rangement? Is he cōntĕnt?' . . . If you could see what these fellows of couriers are when their families are not upon the move, you would feel what a prize he is. I can't make out whether he was ever a smuggler, but nothing will induce him to give the custom-house officers anything: in consequence of which that portmanteau of mine has been unnecessarily opened twenty times. Two of them will come to the coach-door, at the gate of a town. 'Is there anything contraband in this carriage, signore?' 'No, no. There's nothing here. I am an Englishman, and this is my servant.' 'A buono mano signore?' 'Roche' (in English), 'give him something, and get rid of him.' He sits unmoved. 'A buono mano signore?' 'Go along with you!' says the brave C. 'Signore, I am a custom-house officer!' 'Well, then, more shame for you!' – he always makes the same answer. And then he turns to me and says in English: while the custom-house officer's face is a portrait of anguish framed in the coach-window, from his intense desire to know what is being told to his disparagement: 'Datter chip,' shaking his fist at him, 'is greatest tief – and you know it you rascal – as never did en-razh me so, that I cannot bear myself!' I suppose chip to mean chap, but it may include the custom-house officer's father and have some reference to the old block, for anything I distinctly know.

Then came a night journey over the Simplon Pass, a journey of which Dickens wrote a thrilling description.

OVER THE SIMPLON

It was ten o'clock at night when we got to Domo d'Ossola, at the foot of the Pass of the Simplon. But as the moon was shining brightly, and there was not a cloud in the starlit sky, it was no time for going to bed, or going anywhere but on. So, we got a little carriage, after some delay, and began the ascent.

The Simplon Road

It was late in November; and the snow lying four or five feet thick in the beaten road on the summit (in other parts the new drift was already deep), the air was piercing cold. But, the serenity of the night, and the grandeur of the road, with its impenetrable shadows, and deep glooms, and its sudden turns into the shining of the moon and its incessant roar of falling water, rendered the journey more and more sublime at every step.

Soon leaving the calm Italian villages below us, sleeping in the moonlight, the road began to wind among dark trees, and after a time emerged upon a barer region, very steep and toilsome, where the moon shone bright and high. By degrees, the roar of water grew louder; and the stupendous track, after crossing the torrent by a bridge, struck in between two massive perpendicular walls of rock that quite shut out the moonlight, and only left a few stars shining in the narrow strip of sky above. Then, even this was lost, in the thick darkness of a cavern in the rock, through which the way was pierced; the terrible cataract thundering and roaring close below it, and its foam and spray hanging, in a mist, about the entrance. Emerging from this cave, and coming again into the moonlight, and across a dizzy bridge, it crept and twisted upward, through the Gorge of Gondo, savage and grand beyond description, with smooth-fronted precipices, rising up on either hand, and almost meeting overhead. Thus we went, climbing on our rugged way, higher and higher all night, without a moment's weariness: lost in the contemplation of the black rocks, the tremendous heights and depths, the fields of smooth snow lying, in the clefts and hollows, and the fierce torrents thundering headlong down the deep abyss.

Towards daybreak, we came among the snow, where a keen wind was blowing fiercely. Having, with some trouble, awakened the inmates of a wooden house in this solitude: round which the wind was howling dismally, catching up the snow in wreaths and hurling it away: we got some breakfast in a room built of rough timbers, but well warmed by a stove, and well contrived (as it had need to be) for keeping out the bitter storms. A sledge being then made ready, and four horses harnessed to it, we went, ploughing, through the snow. Still upward, but now in the cold light of morning, and with the great white desert on which we travelled, plain and clear.

We were well upon the summit of the mountain: and had before us the rude cross of wood, denoting its greatest altitude above the sea: when the light of the rising sun, struck, all at once, upon the waste of snow, and turned it a deep red. The lonely grandeur of the scene, was then at its height.

As we went sledging on, there came out of the Hospice founded by Napoleon, a group of Peasant travellers, with staves and knapsacks, who had rested there last night: attended by a Monk or two, their hospitable entertainers, trudging slowly forward with them, for company's sake. It was pleasant to give them good morning, and pretty, looking back a long way after them, to see them looking back at us, and hesitating presently, when one of our horses stumbled and fell, whether or no they should return and help us. But he was soon up again, with the assistance of a rough waggoner whose team had stuck fast there too; and when we had helped him out of his difficulty, in return, we left him slowly ploughing towards them, and went softly and swiftly forward, on the brink of a steep precipice, among the mountain pines.

Taking to our wheels again, soon afterwards, we began rapidly to descend; passing under everlasting glaciers, by means of arched galleries, hung with clusters of dripping icicles; under and over foaming waterfalls; near places of refuge, and galleries of shelter against sudden danger; through caverns over whose arched roofs the avalanches slide, in spring, and bury themselves in the unknown gulf beneath. Down, over lofty bridges, and through horrible ravines: a little shifting speck in the vast desolation of ice and snow, and monstrous granite rocks; down through the deep Gorge of the Saltine, and deafened by the torrent plunging madly down, among the riven blocks of rock, into the level country, far below. Gradually down, by zig-zag roads, lying between an upward and a downward precipice, into warmer weather, calmer air, and softer scenery, until there lay before us, glittering like gold or silver in the thaw and sunshine, the metal-covered, red, green, yellow, domes and church-spires of a Swiss town.

On 3 December Dickens gave his promised reading of The Chimes. *The well-known sketch by Maclise shows him – with an appropriate halo – reading in Forster's room to an entranced audience of ten, which included Forster, Stanfield, Maclise, Carlyle and Dickens' own brother Frederick. After the fashion of the time, they had no shyness in weeping copiously as well as roaring with laughter. Two days later Dickens gave a second reading, after which he wrote to his wife: 'If you had seen Macready undisguisedly sobbing and crying on the sofa you would have felt, as I did, what a thing it is to have power'.*

These were in fact the first of those hypnotising performances which later on were to make him so fantastically famous.

Towards Rome

When Forster sympathised with Dickens about the hardships of his past and future journeys, he replied warmly: 'I would not recall an inch of the way to and from you if it had been twenty times as long and ten thousand times as wintry'.

He had need of all such enthusiasm to carry him through a most uncomfortable return, only lightened by a brief stay in Paris where he watched Macready rehearsing Othello. *But he got back to Genoa before Christmas. The new year, 1845, started with a birthday party for his son Charley who was eight on Twelfth Day, made memorable by the present from his godmother, the wealthy and generous Angela Burdet Coutts, of an iced cake weighing seventy-six pounds, which a local cake-shop, where it had been sent for repairs, had exhibited to the wonder of Genoa.*

Dickens and Catherine had planned to take a Spring holiday, centred on Rome but including an interlude in Naples, where Georgina was to meet them and return with them to Rome for Easter Week.

On their journey from Genoa they passed Carrara, with its unforgettable marble quarries.

THE QUARRIES AT CARRARA

The Magra safely crossed in the Ferry Boat – the passage is not by any means agreeable, when the current is swollen and strong – we arrived at Carrara, within a few hours. In good time next morning, we got some ponies, and went out to see the marble quarries.

They are four or five great glens, running up into a range of lofty hills, until they can run no longer, and are stopped by being abruptly strangled by Nature. The quarries, 'or caves,' as they call them there, are so many openings, high up in the hills, on either side of these passes, where they blast and excavate for marble: which may turn out good or bad: may make a man's fortune very quickly, or ruin him by the great expense of working what is worth nothing. Some of these caves were opened by the ancient Romans, and remain as they left them to this hour. Many others are being worked at this moment; others are to be begun to-morrow, next week, next month; others are unbought, unthought of; and marble enough for more ages than have passed since the place was resorted to, lies hidden everywhere: patiently awaiting its time of discovery.

As you toil and clamber up one of these steep gorges (having left your pony soddening his girths in water, a mile or two lower down) you hear, every now and then, echoing among the hills, in a low tone, more silent than the previous silence, a melancholy warning bugle, – a signal to the miners to withdraw. Then, there is a thundering, and echoing from hill to hill, and perhaps a splashing up of great fragments of rock into the air; and on you toil again until some other bugle sounds, in a new direction, and you stop directly, lest you should come within the range of the new explosion.

There were numbers of men, working high up in these hills – on the sides – clearing away, and sending down the broken masses of stone and earth, to make way for the blocks of marble that had been discovered. As these came rolling down from unseen hands into the narrow valley, I could not help thinking of the deep glen (just the same sort of glen) where the Roc left Sindbad the Sailor; and where the merchants from the heights above, flung down great pieces of meat for the diamonds to stick to. There were no eagles here, to darken the sun in their swoop, and pounce upon them; but it was as wild and fierce as if there had been hundreds.

But the road, the road down which the marble comes, however immense the blocks! The genius of the country, and the spirit of its institutions, pave that road: repair it, watch it, keep it going! Conceive a channel of water running over a rocky bed, beset with great heaps of stone of all shapes and sizes, winding down the middle of this valley; and *that* being the road – because it was the road five hundred years ago! Imagine the clumsy carts of five hundred years ago, being used to this hour, and drawn, as they used to be, five hundred years ago, by oxen, whose ancestors were worn to death five hundred years ago, as their unhappy descendants are now, in twelve months, by the suffering and agony of this cruel work! Two pair, four pair, ten pair, twenty pair, to one block, according to its size; down it must come, this way. In their struggling from stone to stone, with their enormous loads behind them, they die frequently upon the spot; and not they alone; for their passionate drivers, sometimes tumbling down in their energy, are crushed to death beneath the wheels. But it was good five hundred years ago, and it must be good now: and a railroad down one of these steeps (the easiest thing in the world) would be flat blasphemy.

When we stood aside, to see one of these cars drawn by only a pair of oxen (for it had but one small block of marble on it), coming down, I hailed, in my heart, the man who sat upon the heavy yoke, to keep it on the neck of the poor beasts – and who faced backwards: not before him – as the very Devil of true despotism. He had a great rod in his hand, with an iron point; and when they could plough and force their way through the loose bed of the torrent no longer, and came to a stop, he poked it into their bodies, beat it on their heads, screwed it round and round in their nostrils, got them on a yard or two, in the madness of intense pain; repeated all these persuasions, with increased intensity of purpose, when they stopped again; got them on, once more; forced and goaded them to an abrupter point of the descent; and when their writhing and smarting, and the weight behind them, bore them plunging down the precipice in a cloud of scattered water, whirled his rod above his head, and gave a great whoop and hallo, as if he had achieved something, and had no idea that they might shake him off, and blindly mash his brains upon the road, in the noon-tide of his triumph.

Standing in one of the many studii of Carrara, that afternoon – for it is a great workshop, full of beautifully-finished copies in marble, of almost every figure, group, and bust, we know – it seemed, at first, so strange to me that those exquisite shapes, replete with grace, and thought, and delicate repose, should grow out of all this toil, and sweat, and torture! But I soon found a parallel to it, and an explanation of it, in every virtue that springs up in miserable ground, and every good thing that has its birth in sorrow and distress. And, looking out of the sculptor's great window, upon the marble mountains, all red and glowing in the decline of day, but stern and solemn to the last, I thought, my God! how many quarries of human hearts and souls, capable of far more beautiful results, are left shut up and mouldering away: while pleasure-travellers through life, avert their faces, as they pass, and shudder at the gloom and ruggedness that conceal them!

The then reigning Duke of Modena, to whom this territory in part belonged, claimed the proud distinction of being the only sovereign in Europe who had not recognised Louis-Philippe as King of the French! He was not a wag, but quite in earnest. He was also much opposed to railroads; and if certain lines in contemplation by other potentates, on either side of him, had been executed, would have probably enjoyed the satisfaction of having an omnibus plying to and fro across his not very vast dominions, to forward travellers from one terminus to another.

Carrara, shut in by great hills, is very picturesque and bold. Few tourists stay there; and the people are nearly all connected, in one way or other, with the working of marble. There are also villages among the caves, where the workmen live. It contains a beautiful little Theatre, newly built; and it is an interesting custom there, to form the chorus of labourers in the marble quarries, who are self-taught and sing by ear. I heard them in a comic opera, and in an act of 'Norma'; and they acquitted themselves very well; unlike the common people of Italy generally, who (with some exceptions among the Neapolitans) sing vilely out of tune, and have very disagreeable singing voices.

Then came Pisa, whose claim, in the light of the Leaning Tower, to be considered 'the seventh wonder of the world' he could not dispute.

PISA

From the summit of a lofty hill beyond Carrara, the first view of the fertile plain in which the town of Pisa lies – with Leghorn, a purple spot in the flat distance – is enchanting. Nor is it only distance that lends enchantment to the view; for the fruitful country, and rich woods of olive-trees through which the road subsequently passes, render it delightful.

The moon was shining when we approached Pisa, and for a long time we could see, behind the wall, the leaning Tower, all awry in the uncertain light; the shadowy original of the old pictures in school-books, setting forth 'The Wonders of the World.' Like most things connected in their first associations with school-books and school-times, it was too small. I felt it keenly. It was nothing like so high above the wall as I had hoped. It was another of the many deceptions practised by Mr Harris, Bookseller, at the corner of St Paul's Churchyard, London. *His* Tower was a fiction, but this was a reality – and, by comparison, a short reality. Still, it looked very well, and very strange, and was quite as much out of the perpendicular as Harris had represented it to be. The quiet air of Pisa too; the big guard-house at the gate, with only two little soldiers in it; the streets with scarcely any show of people in them; and the Arno, flowing quaintly through the centre of the town; were excellent. So, I bore no malice in my heart against Mr Harris (remembering his good intentions), but forgave him before dinner, and went out, full of confidence, to see the Tower next morning.

I might have known better; but, somehow, I had expected to see it, casting its long shadow on a public street where people came and went all day. It was a surprise to me to find it in a grave retired place, apart from the general resort, and carpeted with smooth green turf. But, the group of buildings, clustered on and about this verdant carpet: comprising the Tower, the Baptistery, the Cathedral, and the Church of the Campo Santo: is perhaps the most remarkable and beautiful in the whole world; and from being clustered there, together, away from the ordinary transactions and details of the town, they have a singularly venerable and impressive character. It is the architectural essence of a rich old city, with all its common life and common habitations pressed out, and filtered away.

Simond compares the Tower to the usual pictorial representations in children's books of the Tower of Babel. It is a happy simile, and conveys a better idea of the building than chapters of laboured description. Nothing can exceed the grace and lightness of the structure; nothing can be more remarkable than its general appearance. In the course of the ascent to the top (which is by an easy staircase), the inclination is not very apparent; but, at the summit, it becomes so, and gives one the sensation of being in a ship that has heeled over, through the action of an ebb-tide. The effect *upon the low side*, so to speak – looking over from the gallery, and seeing the shaft recede to its base – is very startling; and I saw a nervous traveller hold on to the Tower involuntarily, after glancing down, as if he had some idea of propping it up. The view within, from the ground – looking up, as through a slanted tube – is also very curious. It certainly inclines as much as the most sanguine tourist could desire. The natural impulse of ninety-nine people out of a hundred, who were about to recline upon the grass below it, to rest, and contemplate the adjacent buildings, would probably be, not to take up their position under the leaning side; it is so very much aslant.

The manifold beauties of the Cathedral and Baptistery need no recapitulation from me; though in this case, as in a hundred others, I find it difficult to separate my own delight in recalling them, from your weariness in having them recalled. There is a picture of St Agnes, by Andrea del Sarto, in the former, and there are a variety of rich columns in the latter, that tempt me strongly.

It is, I hope, no breach of my resolution not to be tempted into elaborate descriptions, to remember the Campo Santo; where grass-grown graves are dug in earth brought more than six hundred years ago, from the Holy Land; and where there are, surrounding them, such cloisters, with such playing lights and shadows falling through their delicate tracery on the stone pavement, as surely the dullest memory could never forget. On the walls of this solemn and lovely place, are ancient frescoes, very much obliterated and decayed, but very curious. As usually happens in almost any collection of paintings, of any sort, in Italy, where there are many heads, there is, in one of them, a striking accidental likeness of Napoleon. At one time, I used to please my fancy with the speculation whether these old painters, at their work, had a foreboding knowledge of the man who would one day arise to wreak such destruction upon art: whose soldiers would make targets of great pictures, and stable their horses among triumphs of architecture. But the same Corsican face is so plentiful in some parts of Italy at this day, that a more commonplace solution of the coincidence is unavoidable.

If Pisa be the seventh wonder of the world in right of its Tower, it may claim to be, at least, the second or third in right of its beggars. They waylay the unhappy visitor at every turn, escort him to every door he enters at, and lie in wait for him, with strong reinforcements, at every door by which they know he must come out. The grating of the portal on its hinges is the signal for a general shout, and the moment he appears, he is hemmed in, and fallen on, by heaps of rags and personal distortions. The beggars seem to embody all the trade and enterprise of Pisa. Nothing else is stirring, but warm air. Going through the streets, the fronts of the sleepy houses look like backs. They are all so still and quiet, and unlike houses with people in them, that the greater part of the city has the appearance of a city at daybreak, or during a general siesta of the population. Or it is yet more like those backgrounds of houses in common prints, or old engravings, where windows and doors are squarely indicated, and one figure (a beggar of course) is seen walking off by itself into illimitable perspective.

But if Pisa had proved to be all that the travellers had expected, they were soon to experience a queer disillusionment. After having travelled for miles across the desolate Campagna Romana, 'an undulating flat where . . . for miles and miles there is nothing to relieve the terrible monotony and gloom . . . we began, in a perfect fever, to strain our eyes for Rome; and when, after another mile or two, the Eternal City appeared, at length, in the distance; it looked like – I am half afraid to write the word – like LONDON!!! *There it lay, under a thick cloud, with innumerable towers, and steeples, and roofs of houses, rising up into the sky, and high above them all, one* Dome. *I swear, that keenly as I felt the seeming absurdity of the comparison, it was so like* London, *that if you had shown it to me in a glass I should have taken it for nothing else.'*

Rome

With what expectations Dickens had come to Rome can only be conjectured. Of one aspect of its history, however, we can be sure he must often have thought. The horrors of religious persecution, of which he had seen so many evidences in dungeons beneath old palaces as well as prisons, had appalled him. In Avignon he had been shown by a hateful old woman he called 'the Goblin' such horrors as make one sick to read about, and in Venice 'such dreadful instruments of torture horribly contrived to cramp, and to pinch, and grind, and crush men's bones, and tear and twist with the torment of a thousand deaths'.

'Past and gone as they are', he wrote to Douglas Jerrold, 'these things stir a man's blood, like a great wrong, or passion of the instant.'

But when he came to the Colosseum, a place which fascinated him so much that he went back there again and again, he was able to write with 'a softened sorrow' even of ancient savageries.

SAINT PETER'S AND THE COLOSSEUM

Immediately on going out next day, we hurried off to St Peter's. It looked immense in the distance, but distinctly and decidedly small, by comparison, on a near approach. The beauty of the Piazza, on which it stands, with its clusters of exquisite columns, and its gushing fountains – so fresh, so broad, and free, and beautiful – nothing can exaggerate. The first burst of the interior, in all its expansive majesty and glory: and, most of all, the looking up into the Dome: is a sensation never to be forgotten. But, there were preparations for a Festa; the pillars of stately marble were swathed in some impertinent frippery of red and yellow; the altar, and entrance to the subterranean chapel:

which is before it: in the centre of the church: were like a goldsmith's shop, or one of the opening scenes in a very lavish pantomime. And though I had as high a sense of the beauty of the building (I hope) as it is possible to entertain, I felt no very strong emotion. I have been infinitely more affected in many English cathedrals when the organ has been playing, and in many English country churches when the congregation have been singing. I had a much greater sense of mystery and wonder, in the Cathedral of San Mark at Venice.

When we came out of the church again (we stood nearly an hour staring up into the dome: and would not have 'gone over' the Cathedral then, for any money), we said to the coachman, 'Go to the Coliseum.' In a quarter of an hour or so, he stopped at the gate, and we went in.

It is no fiction, but plain, sober, honest Truth, to say: so suggestive and distinct is it at this hour: that, for a moment – actually in passing in – they who will, may have the whole great pile before them, as it used to be, with thousands of eager faces staring down into the arena, and such a whirl of strife, and blood, and dust going on there, as no language can describe. Its solitude, its awful beauty, and its utter desolation, strike upon the stranger the next moment, like a softened sorrow; and never in his life, perhaps, will he be so moved and overcome by any sight, not immediately connected with his own affections and afflictions.

To see it crumbling there, an inch a year; its walls and arches overgrown with green; its corridors open to the day; the long grass growing in its porches; young trees of yesterday, springing up on its ragged parapets, and bearing fruit: chance produce of the seeds dropped there by the birds who build their nests within its chinks and crannies; to see its Pit of Fight filled up with earth, and the peaceful Cross planted in the centre; to climb into its upper halls, and look down on ruin, ruin, ruin, all about it; the triumphal arches of Constantine, Septimus Severus, and Titus; the Roman Forum; the Palace of the Cæsars; the temples of the old religion, fallen down and gone; is to see the ghost of old Rome, wicked wonderful old city, haunting the very ground on which its people trod. It is the most impressive, the most stately, the most solemn, grand, majestic, mournful sight, conceivable. Never, in its bloodiest prime, can the sight of the gigantic Coliseum, full and running over with the lustiest life, have moved one heart, as it must move all who look upon it now, a ruin. GOD be thanked: a ruin!

As it tops the other ruins: standing there, a mountain among graves: so do its ancient influences outlive all other remnants of the old mythology and old butchery of Rome, in the nature of the fierce and cruel Roman people. The Italian face changes as the visitor approaches the city; its beauty becomes devilish; and there is scarcely one countenance in a hundred, among the common people in the streets, that would not be at home and happy in a renovated Coliseum to-morrow.

Here was Rome indeed at last; and such a Rome as no one can imagine in its full and awful grandeur! We wandered out upon the Appian Way, and then went on, through miles of ruined tombs and broken walls, with here and there a desolate and uninhabited house: past the Circus of Romulus, where the course of the chariots, the stations of the judges, competitors, and spectators, are yet as plainly to be seen as in old time: past the tomb of Cecilia Metella: past all inclosure, hedge, or stake, wall or fence: away upon the open Campagna, where on that side of Rome, nothing is to be beheld but Ruin. Except where the distant Apennines bound the view upon the left, the whole wide prospect is one field of ruin. Broken aqueducts, left in the most picturesque and beautiful clusters of arches; broken temples; broken tombs. A desert of decay, sombre and desolate beyond all expression; and with a history in every stone that strews the ground.

On Sunday, the Pope assisted in the performance of High Mass at St Peter's. The effect of the Cathedral on my mind, on that second visit, was exactly what it was at first, and what it remains after many visits. It is not religiously impressive or affecting. It is an immense edifice, with no one point for the mind to rest upon; and it tires itself with wandering round and round. The very purpose of the place, is not expressed in anything you see there, unless you examine its details – and all examination of details is incompatible with the place itself. It might be a Pantheon, or a Senate House, or a great architectural trophy, having no other object than an architectural triumph. There is a black statue of St Peter, to be sure, under a red canopy; which is larger than life, and which is constantly having its great toe kissed by good Catholics. You cannot help seeing that: it is so very prominent and popular. But it does not heighten the effect of the temple, as a work of art; and it is not expressive – to me at least – of its high purpose.

A large space behind the altar, was fitted up with boxes, shaped like those at the Italian Opera in England, but in their decoration much more gaudy. In the centre of the kind of theatre thus railed off, was a canopied dais with the Pope's chair upon it. The pavement was covered with a carpet of the brightest green; and what with this green, and the intolerable reds and crimsons, and gold borders of the hangings, the whole concern looked like a stupendous Bonbon. On either side of the altar, was a large box for lady strangers. These were filled with ladies in black dresses and black veils. The gentlemen of the Pope's guard, in red coats, leather breeches, and jack-boots, guarded all this reserved space, with drawn swords that were very flashy in every sense; and from the altar all down the nave, a broad lane was kept clear by the Pope's Swiss guard, who wear a quaint striped surcoat, and striped tight legs, and carry halberds like those which are usually shouldered by those theatrical supernumeraries, who never *can* get off the stage fast enough, and who may be generally observed to linger in the enemy's camp after the open country, held by the opposite forces, has been split up the middle by a convulsion of Nature.

I got upon the border of the green carpet, in company with a great many other gentlemen, attired in black (no other passport is necessary), and stood there at my ease, during the performance of Mass. The singers were in a crib of wirework (like a large meat-safe or bird-cage) in one corner; and sang most atrociously. All about the green carpet, there was a slowly moving crowd of people; talking to each other: staring at the Pope through eye-glasses; defrauding one another, in moments of partial curiosity, out of precarious seats on the bases of pillars: and grinning hideously at the ladies. Dotted here and there, were little knots of friars (Francescáni, or Cappuccíni, in their coarse brown dresses and peaked hoods) making a strange contrast to the gaudy ecclesiastics of higher degree, and having their humility gratified to the utmost, by being shouldered about, and elbowed right and left, on all sides. Some of these had muddy sandals and umbrellas, and stained garments: having trudged in from the country. The faces of the greater part were as coarse and heavy as their dress; their dogged, stupid, monotonous stare at all the glory and splendour, having something in it, half miserable, and half ridiculous.

Upon the green carpet itself, and gathered round the altar, was a perfect army of cardinals and priests, in red, gold, purple, violet, white, and fine linen. Stragglers from these, went to and fro among the crowd, conversing two and two, or giving and receiving introductions, and exchanging salutations; other functionaries in black gowns, and other functionaries in court-dresses, were similarly engaged. In the midst of all these, and stealthy Jesuits creeping in and out, and the extreme restlessness of the Youth of England, who were perpetually wandering about, some few steady persons in black cassocks, who had knelt down with their faces to the wall, and were poring over their missals, became, unintentionally, a sort of humane man-traps, and with their own devout legs, tripped up other people's by the dozen.

There was a great pile of candles lying down on the floor near me, which a very old man in a rusty black gown with an open-work tippet, like a summer ornament for a fireplace in tissue-paper, made himself very busy in dispensing to all the ecclesiastics: one a-piece. They loitered about with these for some time, under their arms like walking-sticks, or in their hands like truncheons. At a certain period of the ceremony, however, each carried his candle up to the Pope, laid it across his two knees to be blessed, took it back again, and filed off. This was done in a very attenuated procession, as you may suppose, and occupied a

The Carnival at Rome–the Chinese Car

long time. Not because it takes long to bless a candle through and through, but because there were so many candles to be blessed. At last they were all blessed; and then they were all lighted; and then the Pope was taken up, chair and all, and carried round the church.

I must say, that I never saw anything, out of November, so like the popular English commemoration of the fifth of that month. A bundle of matches and a lantern, would have made it perfect. Nor did the Pope, himself, at all mar the resemblance, though he has a pleasant and venerable face; for, as this part of the ceremony makes him giddy and sick, he shuts his eyes when it is performed: and having his eyes shut and a great mitre on his head, and his head itself wagging to and fro as they shook him in carrying, he looked as if his mask were going to tumble off. The two immense fans which are always borne, one on either side of him, accompanied him, of course, on this occasion. As they carried him along, he blessed the people with the mystic sign; and as he passed them, they kneeled down. When he had made the round of the church, he was brought back again, and if I am not mistaken, this performance was repeated, in the whole, three times. There was, certainly, nothing solemn or effective in it; and certainly very much that was droll and tawdry. But this remark applies to the whole ceremony, except the raising of the Host, when every man in the guard dropped on one knee instantly, and dashed his naked sword on the ground; which had a fine effect.

The next time I saw the cathedral, was some two or three weeks afterwards, when I climbed up into the ball; and then, the hangings being taken down, and the carpet taken up, but all the framework left, the remnants of these decorations looked like an exploded cracker.

But there was one corner in Rome, physically as different as can be imagined from the great open space of the Colosseum, which left on his sensitive spirit an even deeper impression. This was a small upper chamber in the Mamertine prison in which it was believed that Saint Peter had been confined.

It is all so silent and so close, and tomb-like; and the dungeons below are so black and stealthy, and stagnant, and naked; that this little dark spot becomes a dream within a dream; and in the vision of great churches which come rolling past me like a sea, it is a small wave by itself, that melts into no other wave, and does not flow on with the rest.

In this same letter Dickens sent Forster his breath-taking story of the Roman Carnival, and the hard-featured account of a public execution which, as Sacheverell Sitwell said, 'stays in the memory like a Goya drawing'.

THE CARNIVAL

The Friday and Saturday having been solemn Festa days, and Sunday being always a *dies non* in carnival proceedings, we had looked forward, with some impatience and curiosity, to the beginning of the new week: Monday and Tuesday being the two last and best days of the Carnival.

On the Monday afternoon at one or two o'clock, there began to be a great rattling of carriages into the court-yard of the hotel; a hurrying to and fro of all the servants in it; and now and then, a swift shooting across some doorway or balcony, of a straggling stranger in a fancy dress: not yet sufficiently well used to the same, to wear it with confidence, and defy public opinion. All the carriages were open, and had the linings carefully covered with white cotton or calico, to prevent their proper decorations from being spoiled by the incessant pelting of sugar-plums; and people were packing and cramming into every vehicle as it waited for its occupants, enormous sacks and baskets full of these confétti, together with such heaps of flowers, tied up in little nose-gays, that some carriages were not only brimful of flowers, but literally running over: scattering, at every shake and jerk of the springs, some of their abundance on the ground. Not to be behindhand in these essential particulars, we caused two very respectable sacks of sugar-plums (each about three feet high) and a large clothes-basket full of flowers to be conveyed into our hired barouche, with all speed. And from our place of observation, in one of the upper balconies of the hotel, we contemplated these arrangements with the liveliest satisfaction. The carriages now beginning to take up their company, and move away, we got into ours, and drove off too, armed with little wire masks for our faces; the sugar-plums, like Falstaff's adulterated sack, having lime in their composition.

The Corso is a street a mile long; a street of shops, and palaces, and private houses, sometimes opening into a broad piazza. There are verandahs and balconies, of all shapes and sizes, to almost every house – not on one story alone, but often to one room or another on every story – put there in general with so little order or regularity, that if, year after year, and season after season, it had rained balconies, hailed balconies, snowed balconies, blown balconies, they could scarcely have come into existence in a more disorderly manner.

This is the great fountain-head and focus of the Carnival. But all the streets in which the Carnival is held, being vigilantly kept by dragoons, it is necessary for carriages, in the first instance, to pass, in line, down another thoroughfare, and so come into the Corso at the end remote from the Piázza del Popolo; which is one of its terminations. Accordingly, we fell into the string of coaches, and, for some time, jogged on quietly enough; now crawling on at a very slow walk; now trotting half-a-dozen yards; now backing fifty; and now stopping altogether: as the pressure in front obliged us. If any impetuous carriage dashed out of the rank and clattered forward, with the wild idea of getting on faster, it was suddenly met, or overtaken, by a trooper on horseback, who, deaf as his own drawn sword to all remonstrances, immediately escorted it back to the very end of the row, and made it a dim speck in the remotest perspective. Occasionally, we interchanged a volley of confétti with the carriage next in front, or the carriage next behind; but as yet, this capturing of stray and errant coaches by the military, was the chief amusement.

Presently, we came into a narrow street, where, besides one line of carriages going, there was another line of carriages returning. Here the sugar-plums and the nosegays began to fly about, pretty smartly; and I was fortunate enough to observe one gentleman attired as a Greek warrior, catch a light-whiskered brigand on the nose (he was in the very act of tossing up a bouquet to a young lady in a first-floor window) with a precision that was much applauded by the bystanders. As this victorious Greek was exchanging a facetious remark with a stout gentleman in a doorway – one-half black and one-half white, as if he had been peeled up the middle – who had offered him his congratulations on this achievement, he received an orange from a house-top, full on his left ear, and was much surprised, not to say discomfited. Especially, as he was standing up at the time; and in consequence of the carriage moving on suddenly, at the same moment, staggered ignominiously, and buried himself among his flowers.

Some quarter of an hour of this sort of progress, brought us to the Corso; and anything so gay, so bright, and lively as the whole scene there, it would be difficult to imagine. From all the innumerable balconies: from the remotest and highest, no less than from the lowest and nearest: hangings of bright red, bright green, bright blue, white and gold, were fluttering in the brilliant sunlight. From windows, and from parapets, and tops of houses, streamers of the richest colours, and draperies of the gaudiest and most sparkling hues, were floating out upon the street. The buildings seemed to have been literally turned inside out, and to have all their gaiety towards the highway. Shop-fronts were taken down, and the windows filled with company, like boxes at a shining theatre; doors were carried off their hinges, and long tapestried groves, hung with garlands of flowers and evergreens, displayed within; builder's scaffoldings were gorgeous temples, radiant in silver, gold, and crimson; and in every nook and corner, from the pavement to the chimney-tops, where women's eyes could glisten, there they danced, and laughed, and sparkled, like the light in water. Every sort of bewitching madness of dress was there. Little preposterous scarlet jackets; quaint old stomachers, more wicked than the smartest bodices; Polish pelisses, strained and tight as ripe gooseberries; tiny Greek caps, all awry, and clinging to the dark hair, Heaven knows how;

every wild, quaint, bold, shy, pettish, madcap fancy had its illustration in a dress; and every fancy was as dead forgotten by its owner, in the tumult of merriment, as if the three old aqueducts that still remain entire had brought Lethe into Rome, upon their sturdy arches, that morning.

The carriages were now three abreast; in broader places four; often stationary for a long time together; always one close mass of variegated brightness; showing, the whole streetful, through the storm of flowers, like flowers of a larger growth themselves. In some, the horses were richly caparisoned in magnificent trappings; in others they were decked from head to tail, with flowing ribbons. Some were driven by coachmen with enormous double faces: one face leering at the horses: the other cocking its extraordinary eyes into the carriage: and both rattling again, under the hail of sugar-plums. Other drivers were attired as women, wearing long ringlets and no bonnets, and looking more ridiculous in any real difficulty with the horses (of which, in such a concourse, there were a great many) than tongue can tell, or pen describe. Instead of sitting *in* the carriages, upon the seats, the handsome Roman women, to see and to be seen the better, sit in the heads of the barouches, at this time of general licence, with their feet upon the cushions – and oh the flowing skirts and dainty waists, the blessed shapes and laughing faces, the free, good-humoured, gallant figures that they make! There were great vans, too, full of handsome girls – thirty, or more together, perhaps – and the broadsides that were poured into, and poured out of, these fairy fire-shops, splashed the air with flowers and bon-bons for ten minutes at a time. Carriages, delayed long in one place, would begin a deliberate engagement with other carriages, or with people at the lower windows; and the spectators at some upper balcony or window, joining in the fray, and attacking both parties, would empty down great bags of confétti, that descended like a cloud, and in an instant made them white as millers. Still, carriages on carriages, dresses on dresses, colours on colours, crowds upon crowds, without end. Men and boys clinging to the wheels of coaches, and holding on behind, and following in their wake, and diving in among the horses' feet to pick up scattered flowers to sell again; maskers on foot (the drollest generally) in fantastic exaggerations of court-dresses, surveying the throng through enormous eye-glasses, and always transported with an ecstasy of love, on the discovery of any particularly old lady at a window; long strings of Policinelli, laying about them with blown bladders at the ends of sticks; a waggonful of madmen, screaming and tearing to the life; a coachful of grave Mamelukes, with their horse-tail standard set up in the midst; a party of gipsy-women engaged in terrific conflict with a shipful of sailors; a man-monkey on a pole, surrounded by strange animals with pigs' faces, and lions' tails, carried under their arms, or worn gracefully over their shoulders; carriages on carriages, dresses on dresses, colours on colours, crowds upon crowds, without end. Not many actual characters sustained, or represented, perhaps, considering the number dressed, but the main pleasure of the scene consisting in its perfect good temper; in its bright, and infinite, and flashing variety; and in its entire abandonment to the mad humour of the time – an abandonment so perfect, so contagious, so irresistible, that the steadiest foreigner fights up to his middle in flowers and sugar-plums, like the wildest Roman of them all, and thinks of nothing else till half-past four o'clock, when he is suddenly reminded (to his great regret) that this is not the whole business of his existence, by hearing the trumpets sound, and seeing the dragoons begin to clear the street.

How it ever *is* cleared for the race that takes place at five, or how the horses ever go through the race, without going over the people, is more than I can say. But the carriages get out into the by-streets, or up into the Piázza del Popolo, and some people sit in temporary galleries in the latter place, and tens of thousands line the Corso on both sides, when the horses are brought out into the Piázza – to the foot of that same column which, for centuries, looked down upon the games and chariot-races in the Circus Maximus.

At a given signal they are started off. Down the live lane, the whole length of the Corso, they fly like the wind: riderless, as all the world knows: with shining ornaments upon their backs, and twisted in their plaited manes: and with heavy little balls stuck full of spikes, dangling at their sides, to goad them on. The jingling of these trappings, and the rattling of their hoofs upon the hard stones; the dash and fury of their speed along the echoing street; nay, the very cannon that are fired – these noises are nothing to the roaring of the multitude: their shouts: the clapping of their hands. But it is soon over – almost instantaneously. More cannon shake the town. The horses have plunged into the carpets put across the street to stop them; the goal is reached; the prizes are won (they are given, in part, by the poor Jews, as a compromise for not running foot-races themselves); and there is an end to that day's sport.

A PUBLIC EXECUTION

On one Saturday morning (the eighth of March), a man was beheaded here. Nine or ten months before, he had waylaid a Bavarian countess, travelling as a pilgrim to Rome – alone and on foot, of course – and performing, it is said, that act of piety for the fourth time. He saw her change a piece of gold at Viterbo, where he lived; followed her; bore her company on her journey for some forty miles or more, on the treacherous pretext of protecting her; attacked her, in the fulfilment of his unrelenting purpose, on the Campagna, within a very short distance of Rome, near to what is called (but what is not) the Tomb of Nero; robbed her; and beat her to death with her own pilgrim's staff. He was newly married, and gave some of her apparel to his wife: saying that he had bought it at a fair. She, however, who had seen the pilgrim-countess passing through their town, recognised some trifle as having belonged to her. Her husband then told her what he had done. She, in confession, told a priest; and the man was taken, within four days after the commission of the murder.

There are no fixed times for the administration of justice, or its execution, in this unaccountable country; and he had been in prison ever since. On the Friday, as he was dining with the other prisoners, they came and told him he was to be beheaded next morning, and took him away. It is very unusual to execute in Lent; but his crime being a very bad one, it was deemed advisable to make an example of him at that time, when great numbers of pilgrims were coming towards Rome, from all parts, for the Holy Week. I heard of this on the Friday evening, and saw the bills up at the churches, calling on the people to pray for the criminal's soul. So, I determined to go, and see him executed.

The beheading was appointed for fourteen and a-half o'clock, Roman time: or a quarter before nine in the forenoon. I had two friends with me; and as we did not know but that the crowd might be very great, we were on the spot by half-past seven. The place of execution was near the church of San Giovanni decolláto (a doubtful compliment to Saint John the Baptist) in one of the impassable back streets without any footway, of which a great part of Rome is composed – a street of rotten houses, which do not seem to belong to anybody, and do not seem to have ever been inhabited, and certainly were never built on any plan, or for any particular purpose, and have no window-sashes, and are a little like deserted breweries, and might be warehouses but for having nothing in them. Opposite to one of these, a white house, the scaffold was built. An untidy, unpainted, uncouth, crazy-looking thing of course: some seven feet high, perhaps: with a tall, gallows-shaped frame rising above it, in which was the knife, charged with a ponderous mass of iron, all ready to descend, and glittering brightly in the morning sun, whenever it looked out, now and then, from behind a cloud.

There were not many people lingering about; and these were kept at a considerable distance from the scaffold, by parties of the Pope's dragoons. Two or three hundred foot-soldiers were under arms, standing at ease in clusters here and there; and the officers were walking up and down in twos and threes, chatting together, and smoking cigars.

At the end of the street, was an open space, where there would be a dust-heap, and piles of broken crockery, and mounds of vegetable refuse, but for such things being thrown anywhere and everywhere in Rome, and favouring no particular sort of locality. We got into a kind of wash-house, belonging to a dwelling-house on this spot; and standing there in an old cart, and on a heap of cart-wheels piled against the wall, looked, through a large grated window, at the scaffold, and straight down the street beyond it, until, in consequence of its turning off abruptly to the left, our perspective was brought to a sudden termination, and had a corpulent officer, in a cocked hat, for its crowning feature.

Nine o'clock struck, and ten o'clock struck, and nothing happened. All the bells of all the churches rang as usual. A little parliament of dogs assembled in the open space, and chased each other, in and out among the soldiers. Fierce-looking Romans of the lowest class, in blue cloaks, russet cloaks, and rags uncloaked, came and went, and talked together. Women and children fluttered, on the skirts of the scanty crowd. One large muddy spot was left quite bare, like a bald place on a man's head. A cigar-merchant, with an earthen pot of charcoal ashes in one hand, went up and down, crying his wares. A pastry-merchant divided his attention between the scaffold and his customers. Boys tried to climb up walls, and tumbled down again. Priests and monks elbowed a passage for themselves among the people, and stood on tiptoe for a sight of the knife: then went away. Artists, in inconceivable hats of the middle-ages, and beards (thank Heaven!) of no age at all, flashed picturesque scowls about them from their stations in the throng. One gentleman (connected with the fine arts, I presume) went up and down in a pair of Hessian-boots, with a red beard hanging down on his breast, and his long and bright red hair, plaited into two tails, one on either side of his head, which fell over his shoulders in front of him, very nearly to his waist, and were carefully entwined and braided!

Eleven o'clock struck; and still nothing happened. A rumour got about, among the crowd, that the criminal would not confess; in which case, the priests would keep him until the Ave Maria (sunset); for it is their merciful custom never finally to turn the crucifix away from a man at that pass, as one refusing to be shriven, and consequently a sinner abandoned of the Saviour, until then. People began to drop off. The officers shrugged their shoulders and looked doubtful. The dragoons, who came riding up below our window, every now and then, to order an unlucky hackney-coach or cart away, as soon as it had comfortably established itself, and was covered with exulting people (but never before), became imperious, and quick-tempered. The bald place hadn't a straggling hair upon it; and the corpulent officer, crowning the perspective, took a world of snuff.

Suddenly, there was a noise of trumpets. 'Attention!' was among the foot-soldiers instantly. They were marched up to the scaffold and formed round it. The dragoons galloped to their nearer stations too. The guillotine became the centre of a wood of bristling bayonets and shining sabres. The people closed round nearer, on the flank of the soldiery. A long straggling stream of men and boys, who had accompanied the procession from the prison, came pouring into the open space. The bald spot was scarcely distinguishable from the rest. The cigar and pastry-merchants resigned all thoughts of business, for the moment, and abandoning themselves wholly to pleasure, got good situations in the crowd. The perspective ended, now, in a troop of dragoons. And the corpulent officer, sword in hand, looked hard at a church close to him, which he could see, but we, the crowd, could not.

After a short delay, some monks were seen approaching to the scaffold from this church; and above their heads, coming on slowly and gloomily, the effigy of Christ upon the cross, canopied with black. This was carried round the foot of the scaffold, to the front, and turned towards the criminal, that he might see it to the last. It was hardly in its place, when he appeared on the platform, bare-footed; his hands bound; and with the collar and neck of his shirt cut away, almost to the shoulder. A young man – six-and-twenty – vigorously made, and well-shaped. Face pale; small dark moustache; and dark brown hair.

He had refused to confess, it seemed, without first having his wife brought to see him; and they had sent an escort for her, which had occasioned the delay.

He immediately kneeled down, below the knife. His neck fitting into a hole, made for the purpose, in a cross plank, was shut down, by another plank above; exactly like the pillory. Immediately below him was a leathern bag. And into it his head rolled instantly.

The executioner was holding it by the hair, and walking with it round the scaffold, showing it to the people, before one quite knew that the knife had fallen heavily, and with a rattling sound.

When it had travelled round the four sides of the scaffold, it was set upon a pole in front – a little patch of black and white, for the long street to stare at, and the flies to settle on. The eyes were turned upward, as if he had avoided the sight of the leathern bag, and looked to the crucifix. Every tinge and hue of life had left it in that instant. It was dull, cold, livid, wax. The body also.

There was a great deal of blood. When we left the window, and went close up to the scaffold, it was very dirty; one of the two men who were throwing water over it, turning to help the other lift the body into a shell, picked his way as through mire. A strange appearance was the apparent annihilation of the neck. The head was taken off so close, that it seemed as if the knife had narrowly escaped crushing the jaw, or shaving off the ear; and the body looked as if there were nothing left above the shoulder.

Nobody cared, or was at all affected. There was no manifestation of disgust, or pity, or indignation, or sorrow. My empty pockets were tried, several times, in the crowd immediately below the scaffold, as the corpse was being put into its coffin. It was an ugly, filthy, careless, sickening spectacle; meaning nothing but butchery beyond the momentary interest, to the one wretched actor. Yes! Such a sight has one meaning and one warning. Let me not forget it. The speculators in the lottery, station themselves at favourable points for counting the gouts of blood that spirt out, here or there; and buy that number. It is pretty sure to have a run upon it.

The body was carted away in due time, the knife cleansed, the scaffold taken down, and all the hideous apparatus removed. The executioner: an outlaw *ex officio* (what a satire on the Punishment!) who dare not, for his life, cross the Bridge of St. Angelo but to do his work: retreated to his lair, and the show was over.

As might have been expected, one of the other sights of 'The Eternal City' that made a deep impression on Dickens was the catacombs.

THE CATACOMBS

It is an awful thing to think of the enormous caverns that are entered from some Roman churches, and undermine the city. Many churches have crypts and subterranean chapels of great size, which, in the ancient time, were baths, and secret chambers of temples, and what not; but I do not speak of them. Beneath the church of St Giovanni and St Paolo, there are the jaws of a terrific range of caverns, hewn out of the rock, and said to have another outlet underneath the Coliseum – tremendous darknesses of vast extent, half-buried in the earth and unexplorable, where the dull torches, flashed by the attendants, glimmer down long ranges of distant vaults branching to the right and left, like streets in a city of the dead; and show the cold damp stealing down the walls, drip-drop, drip-drop, to join the pools of water that lie here and there, and never saw, or never will see, one ray of the sun. Some accounts make these the prisons of the wild beasts destined for the amphitheatre; some the prisons of the condemned gladiators; some, both. But the legend most appalling to the fancy is, that in the upper range (for there are two stories of these caves) the Early Christians destined to be eaten at the Coliseum Shows, heard the wild beasts, hungry for them, roaring down below; until, upon the night and solitude of their captivity, there burst the sudden noon and life of the vast theatre crowded to the parapet, and of these, their dreaded neighbours, bounding in!

Below the church of San Sebastiano, two miles beyond the gate of San Sebastiano, on the Appian Way, is the entrance to the catacombs of Rome – quarries in the old time, but afterwards the hiding-places of the Christians. These ghastly passages have been explored for twenty miles; and form a chain of labyrinths, sixty miles in circumference.

A gaunt Franciscan friar, with a wild bright eye, was our only guide, down into this profound and dreadful place. The narrow ways and openings hither and thither, coupled with the dead and heavy air, soon blotted out, in all of us, any recollection of the track by which we had come: and I could not help thinking 'Good

Heaven, if, in a sudden fit of madness, he should dash the torches out, or if he should be seized with a fit, what would become of us!' On we wandered, among martyrs' graves: passing great subterranean vaulted roads, diverging in all directions, and choked up with heaps of stones, that thieves and murderers may not take refuge there, and form a population under Rome, even worse than that which lives between it and the sun. Graves, graves, graves; Graves of men, of women, of their little children, who ran crying to the persecutors, 'We are Christians! We are Christians!' that they might be murdered with their parents; Graves with the palm of martyrdom roughly cut into their stone boundaries, and little niches, made to hold a vessel of the martyrs' blood; Graves of some who lived down here, for years together, ministering to the rest, and preaching truth, and hope, and comfort, from the rude altars, that bear witness to their fortitude at this hour; more roomy graves, but far more terrible, where hundreds, being surprised, were hemmed in and walled up: buried before Death, and killed by slow starvation.

'The Triumphs of the Faith are not above ground in our splendid churches,' said the friar, looking round upon us, as we stopped to rest in one of the low passages, with bones and dust surrounding us on every side. 'They are here! Among the Martyrs' Graves!' He was a gentle, earnest man, and said it from his heart; but when I thought how Christian men have dealt with one another; how, perverting our most merciful religion, they have hunted down and tortured, burnt and beheaded, strangled, slaughtered, and oppressed each other; I pictured to myself an agony surpassing any that this Dust had suffered with the breath of life yet lingering in it, and how these great and constant hearts would have been shaken – how they would have quailed and drooped – if a foreknowledge of the deeds that professing Christians would commit in the Great Name for which they died, could have rent them with its own unutterable anguish, on the cruel wheel, and bitter cross, and in the fearful fire.

Dickens made no pretensions to any real knowledge of the visual arts, but by now, having viewed hundreds of pictures, he had come to the conclusion that there was a great deal too much 'cant' among artists and their devotees, and a wearisome obviousness about all the 'rules'. To him the subject-matter was of prime importance, and he refused to admire paintings, however famous, which failed to appeal to him. How, he asked, could anyone who loved Titian's 'Assumption of the Virgin' and Tintoretto's 'Assembly of the Blessed' find in Michelangelo's 'Last Judgment' 'any general idea or one pervading thought, in harmony with the stupendous subject?' But he also wrote:

There are portraits innumerable by Titian, Rubens, Rembrandt and Vandyke; heads by Guido, and Domenichino, and Carlo Dolci; subjects by Raphael and Correggio and Murillo, and Paul Veronese, and Salvater; which it would be difficult indeed to praise too highly, or to praise enough . . . Such tenderness, and grace, such noble elevation, purity and beauty so shine upon me from some well-remembered spots in the walls of those galleries, as to relieve my tortured memory from legions of whining friars and waxy holy families.

The models who hung about on the Spanish Steps in Rome, waiting to be hired, seemed strangely familiar to him, and one day he realised that they had all figured in the paintings he had seen in the Royal Academy in London. Here, of course, were 'the venerable model, the Pastoral model, the assassin model' whom young students copied again and again, 'finding nothing fresh or suggestive in the world about them'.

Naples

In and around Naples, as in Rome, it was of the dramatic contrasts that Dickens was most aware.

THE BEGGARS OF FONDI

The Neapolitan frontier crossed, after two hours' travelling; and the hungriest of soldiers and custom-house officers with difficulty appeased; we enter, by a gateless portal, into the first Neapolitan town – Fondi. Take note of Fondi, in the name of all that is wretched and beggarly.

A filthy channel of mud and refuse meanders down the centre of the miserable streets, fed by obscene rivulets that trickle from the abject houses. There is not a door, a window, or a shutter; not a roof, a wall, a post, or a pillar, in all Fondi, but is decayed, and crazy, and rotting away. The wretched history of the town, with all its sieges and pillages by Barbarossa and the rest, might have been acted last year. How the gaunt dogs that sneak about the miserable streets, come to be alive, and undevoured by the people, is one of the enigmas of the world.

A hollow-cheeked and scowling people they are! All beggars; but that's nothing. Look at them as they gather round. Some, are too indolent to come downstairs, or are too wisely mistrustful of the stairs, perhaps, to venture: so stretch out their lean hands from upper windows, and howl; others, come flocking about us, fighting and jostling one another, and demanding, incessantly, charity for the love of God, charity for the love of the Blessed Virgin, charity for the love of all the Saints. A group of miserable children, almost naked, screaming forth the same petition, discover that they can see themselves reflected in the varnish of the carriage, and begin to dance and make grimaces, that they may have the pleasure of seeing their antics repeated in this mirror. A crippled idiot, in the act of striking one of them who drowns his clamorous demand for charity, observes his angry counterpart in the panel, stops short, and thrusting out his tongue, begins to wag his head and chatter. The shrill cry raised at this, awakens half-a-dozen wild creatures wrapped in frowzy brown cloaks, who are lying on the church-steps with pots and pans for sale. These, scrambling up, approach, and beg defiantly. 'I am hungry. Give me something. Listen to me, Signor. I am hungry!' Then, a ghastly old woman, fearful of being too late, comes hobbling down the street, stretching out one hand, and scratching herself all the way with the other, and screaming, long before she can be heard, 'Charity, charity! I'll go and pray for you directly, beautiful lady, if you'll give me charity!' Lastly, the members of a brotherhood for burying the dead: hideously masked, and attired in shabby black robes, white at the skirts, with the splashes of many muddy winters: escorted by a dirty priest, and a congenial cross-bearer: come hurrying past. Surrounded by this motley concourse, we move out of Fondi: bad bright eyes glaring at us, out of the darkness of every crazy tenement, like glistening fragments of its filth and putrefaction.

THE CITY OF NAPLES

A noble mountain-pass, with the ruins of a fort on a strong eminence, traditionally called the Fort of Fra Diavolo; the old town of Itrí, like a device in pastry, built up, almost perpendicularly, on a hill, and approached by long steep flights of steps; beautiful Mola di Gaëta, whose wines, like those of Albano, have degenerated since the days of Horace, or his taste for wine was bad: which is not likely of one who enjoyed it so much, and extolled it so well; another night upon the road at St Agatha; a rest next day at Capua, which is picturesque, but hardly so seductive to a traveller now, as the soldiers of Prætorian Rome were wont to find the ancient city of that name; a flat road among vines festooned and looped from tree to tree; and Mount Vesu-

Dickens, his wife Catherine, and her sister
Georgina Hogarth

vius close at hand at last! – its cone and summit whitened with snow; and its smoke hanging over it, in the heavy atmosphere of the day, like a dense cloud. So we go, rattling down hill, into Naples.

A funeral is coming up the street, towards us. The body, on an open bier, borne on a kind of palanquin, covered with a gay cloth of crimson and gold. The mourners, in white gowns and masks. If there be death abroad, life is well represented too, for all Naples would seem to be out of doors, and tearing to and fro in carriages. Some of these, the common Vetturíno vehicles, are drawn by three horses abreast, decked with smart trappings and great abundance of brazen ornament, and always going very fast. Not that their loads are light; for the smallest of them has at least six people inside, four in front, four or five more hanging on behind, and two or three more, in a net or bag below the axle-tree, where they lie half-suffocated with mud and dust. Exhibitors of Punch, buffo singers with guitars, reciters of poetry, reciters of stories, a row of cheap exhibitions with clowns and showmen, drums, and trumpets, painted cloths representing the wonders within, and admiring crowds assembled without, assist the whirl and bustle. Ragged lazzaroni lie asleep in doorways, archways, and kennels; the gentry, gaily dressed are dashing up and down in carriages on the Chiaja, or walking in the Public Gardens; and quiet letter-writers, perched behind their little desks and inkstands under the Portico of the Great Theatre of San Carlo, in the public street, are waiting for clients.

Here is a galley-slave in chains, who wants a letter written to a friend. He approaches a clerkly-looking man, sitting under the corner arch, and makes his bargain. He has obtained permission of the sentinel who guards him: who stands near, leaning against the wall and cracking nuts. The galley-slave dictates in the ear of the letter-writer, what he desires to say; and as he can't read writing, looks intently in his face, to read there whether he sets down faithfully what he is told. After a time, the galley-slave becomes discursive – incoherent. The secretary pauses and rubs his chin. The galley-slave is voluble and energetic. The secretary, at length, catches the idea, and with the air of a man who knows how to word it, sets it down; stopping, now and then, to glance back at his text admiringly. The galley-slave is silent. The soldier stoically cracks his nuts. Is there anything more to say? inquires the letter-writer. No more. Then listen, friend of mine. He reads it through. The galley-slave is quite enchanted. It is folded, and addressed, and given to him, and he pays the fee. The secretary falls back indolently in his chair, and takes a book. The galley-slave gathers up an empty sack. The sentinel throws away a handful of nut-shells shoulders his musket, and away they go together.

Why do the beggars rap their chins constantly, with their right hands, when you look at them? Everything is done in pantomime in Naples, and that is the conventional sign for hunger. A man who is quarrelling with another, yonder, lays the palm of his right hand on the back of his left, and shakes the two thumbs – expressive of a donkey's ears – whereat his adversary is goaded to desperation. Two people bargaining for fish, the buyer empties an imaginary waistcoat pocket when he is told the price, and walks away without a word: having thoroughly conveyed to the seller that he considers it too dear. Two people in carriages, meeting, one touches his lips, twice or thrice, holding up the five fingers of his right hand, and gives a horizontal cut in the air with the palm. The other nods briskly, and goes his way. He has been invited to a friendly dinner at half-past five o'clock, and will certainly come.

All over Italy, a peculiar shake of the right hand from the wrist, with the forefinger stretched out, expresses a negative – the only negative beggars will ever understand. But, in Naples, those five fingers are a copious language.

All this, and every other kind of our-door life and stir, and maccaroni-eating at sunset, and flower-selling all day long, and begging and stealing everywhere and at all hours, you see upon the bright sea-shore, where the waves of the bay sparkle merrily. But, lovers and hunters of the picturesque, let us not keep too studiously out of view the miserable depravity, degradation, and wretchedness, with which this gay Neapolitan life is inseparably associated! It is not well to find Saint Giles's so repulsive, and the Porta Capuana so attractive. A pair of naked legs and a ragged red scarf, do not make *all* the difference between what is interesting and what is coarse and odious? Painting and poetising for ever, if you will, the beauties of this most beautiful and lovely spot of earth, let us, as our duty, try to associate a new picturesque with some faint recognition of man's destiny and capabilities; more hopeful, I believe, among the ice and snow of the North Pole, than in the sun and bloom of Naples.

On 17 February, Dickens (accompanied by his long-suffering wife) made the ascent of Vesuvius, and he later sent a hair-raising account of the expedition to his friend Mitton.

ASCENDING VESUVIUS

Yesterday evening, at four o'clock, we began (a small party of six) the ascent of Mount Vesuvius, with six saddle-horses, an armed soldier for a guard, and twenty-two guides. The latter rendered necessary by the severity of the weather, which is greater than has been known for twenty years, and has covered the precipitous part of the mountain with deep snow, the surface of which is glazed with one smooth sheet of ice from the top of the cone to the bottom. By starting at that hour I intended to get the sunset about halfway up, and night at the top, where the fire is raging. It was an inexpressibly lovely night without a cloud; and when the day was quite gone, the moon (within a few hours of the full) came proudly up, showing the sea, and the Bay of Naples, and the whole country, in such majesty as no words can express. We rode to the beginning of the snow and then dismounted. Catherine and Georgina were put into two litters, just chairs with poles, like those in use in England on the 5th of November; and a fat Englishman, who was of the party, was hoisted into a third, borne by eight men. I was accommodated with a tough stick, and we began to plough our way up. The ascent was as steep as this line / – very nearly perpendicular. We were all tumbling at every step; and looking up and seeing the people in advance tumbling over one's very head, and looking down and seeing hundreds of feet of smooth ice below, was, I must confess, anything but agreeable. However, I knew there was little chance of another clear night before I leave this, and gave the word to get up, somehow or other. So on we went, winding a little now and then, or we should not have got on at all. By prodigious exertions we passed the region of snow, and came into that of fire – desolate and awful, you may well suppose. It was like working one's way through a dry waterfall, with every mass of Stone burnt and charred into enormous cinders, and smoke and sulphur bursting out of every chink and crevice, so that it was difficult to breathe. High before us, bursting out of a hill at the top of the mountain, shaped like this A, the fire was pouring out, reddening the night with flames, blackening it with smoke, and spotting it with red-hot stones and cinders that fell down again in showers. At every step everybody fell, now into a hot chink, now into a bed of ashes, now over a mass of cindered iron; and the confusion in the darkness (for the smoke obscured the moon in this part), and the quarrelling and shouting and roaring of the guides, and the waiting every now and then for somebody who was not to be found, and was supposed to have stumbled into some pit or other, made such a scene of it as I can give you no idea of. My ladies were now on foot, of course; but we dragged them on as well as we could (they were thorough game, and didn't make the least complaint), until we got to the foot of that topmost hill I have drawn so beautifully. Here we all stopped; but the head guide, an English gentleman of the name of Le Gros – who has been here many years, and has been up the mountain a hundred times – and your humble servant, resolved (like jackasses) to climb that hill to the brink, and look down into the crater itself. You may form some notion of what is going on inside it, when I tell you that it is a hundred feet higher than it was six weeks ago. The sensation of struggling up it, choked with the fire and smoke, and feeling at every step as if the crust of ground between one's feet and the gulf of fire would crumble in and swallow one up (which is the real danger), I shall remember for some little time, I think. But we did it. We looked down into the flaming bowels of the mountain and came back again, alight in half-a-dozen places, and burnt from head to foot. You never saw such devils. And *I* never saw anything so awful and terrible.

Roche had been tearing his hair like a madman, and crying that we should all three be killed, which made the rest of the company very comfortable, as you may suppose. But we had some wine in a basket, and all swallowed a little of that and a great deal of sulphur before we began to descend. The usual way, after the fiery part is past – you will understand that to be all the flat top of the mountain, in the centre of which, again, rises the little hill I have drawn – is to slide down the ashes, which, slipping from under you, make a gradually increasing ledge under your feet, and prevent your going too fast. But when we came to this steep place last night, we found nothing there but one smooth solid sheet of ice. The only way to get down was for the guides to make a chain, holding by each other's hands, and beat a narrow track in it into the snow below with their sticks. My two unfortunate ladies were taken out of their litters again, with half-a-dozen men hanging on to each, to prevent their falling forward; and we began to descend this way. It was like a tremendous dream. It was impossible to stand, and the only way to prevent oneself from going sheer down the precipice, every time one fell, was to drive one's stick into one of the holes the guides had made, and hold on by that. Nobody could pick one up, or stop one, or render one the least assistance. Now, conceive my horror, when this Mr Le Gros I have mentioned, being on one side of Georgina and I on the other, suddenly staggers away from the narrow path on to the smooth ice, gives us a jerk, lets go, and plunges headforemost down the smooth ice into the black night, five hundred feet below! Almost at the same instant, a man far behind, carrying a light basket on his head with some of our spare cloaks in it, misses his footing and rolls down in another place; and after him, rolling over and over like a black bundle, goes a boy, shrieking as nobody but an Italian can shriek, until the breath is tumbled out of him.

The Englishman is in bed to-day, terribly bruised but without any broken bones. He was insensible at first and a mere heap of rags; but we got him before the fire, in a little hermitage there is halfway down, and he so far recovered as to be able to take some supper, which was waiting for us there. The boy was brought in with his head tied up in a bloody cloth, about half an hour after the rest of us were assembled. And the man who had had the basket was not found when we left the mountain at midnight. What became of the cloaks (mine was among them) I know as little. My ladies' clothes were so torn off their backs that they would not have been decent, if there could have been any thought of such things at such a time. And when we got down to the guides' house, we found a French surgeon (one of another party who had been up before us) lying on a bed in a stable, with God knows what horrible breakage about him, but suffering acutely and looking like death. A pretty unusual trip for a pleasure expedition, I think!

I am rather stiff to-day but am quite unhurt, except a slight scrape on my right hand. My clothes are burnt to pieces. My ladies are the wonder of Naples, and everybody is open-mouthed.

A Secret Expedition

While returning from Rome to the Palazzo Peschiere, Dickens visited Florence, a city which thereafter he remembered, with Genoa and Venice, as one of the three most beautiful in Northern Italy.

But now, in the few weeks of early summer before he was due to go back to England, he made one expedition which, for political reasons, he knew he must not describe even in private letters. It was not until 1860 that 'The Uncommercial' revealed some of his own part in the true story of 'The Italian Prisoner'. And even at that date the prisoner's real name and that of his place of residence was still withheld.

Before he had come out to Genoa, Dickens had made friends with Mazzini, the noble Italian patriot who had lived in exile in England since 1836. He had inspired and led a group called 'Young Italy' whose object was to revolutionise the whole condition of Italy by unifying all those small states – naturally one – whose differences and discords had given France and Austria so many opportunities for their constant invasions, occupations and abominable oppressions of all the Italian people. From England, nevertheless, Mazzini continued to be the guiding spirit of 'Young Italy', and many liberal-minded Englishmen, including Carlyle, Dickens, Forster, Thackeray and Douglas Jerrold, supported him.

Four years later – in 1849 – they were to issue an Appeal On Behalf Of The Italian Refugees, *drawn up by Dickens and published in* The Examiner. *At this moment, in 1845, one of their chief supporters was Lord Dudley Coutts Stuart, 'the Englishman' who is the central figure in 'The Italian Prisoner'. Dickens tells with rare economy and directness this moving tale of how, in fulfillment of his promise to 'the Englishman', he sought out an ex-political prisoner whom that generous man had befriended.*

THE ITALIAN PRISONER

The rising of the Italian people from under their unutterable wrongs, and the tardy burst of day upon them after the long long night of oppression that has darkened their beautiful country, have naturally caused my mind to dwell often of late on my own small wanderings in Italy. Connected with them, is a curious little drama, in which the character I myself sustained was so very subordinate that I may relate its story without any fear of being suspected of self-display. It is strictly a true story.

I am newly arrived one summer evening, in a certain small town on the Mediterranean. I have had my dinner at the inn, and I and the mosquitoes are coming out into the streets together. It is far from Naples; but a bright brown plump little woman-servant at the inn, is a Neapolitan, and is so vivaciously expert in pantomimic action, that in the single moment of answering my request to have a pair of shoes cleaned which I have left up-stairs, she plies imaginary brushes, and goes completely through the motions of polishing the shoes up, and laying them at my feet. I smile at the brisk little woman in perfect satisfaction with her briskness; and the brisk little woman, amiably pleased with me because I am pleased with her, claps her hands and laughs delightfully. We are in the inn yard. As the little woman's bright eyes sparkle on the cigarette I am smoking, I make bold to offer her one; she accepts it none the less merrily, because I touch a most charming little dimple in her fat cheek, with its light paper end. Glancing up at the many green lattices to assure herself that the mistress is not looking on, the little woman then puts her two little dimple arms a-kimbo, and stands on tiptoe to light her cigarette at mine. 'And now, dear little sir,' says she, puffing out smoke in a most innocent and cherubic manner, 'keep quite straight on, take the first to the right, and probably you will see him standing at his door.'

I have a commission to 'him', and I have been inquiring about him. I have carried the commission about Italy several months. Before I left England, there came to me one night a certain generous and gentle English nobleman (he is dead in these days when I relate the story, and exiles have lost their best British friend), with this request: 'Whenever you come to such a town, will you seek out one Giovanni Carlavero, who keeps a little wine-shop there, mention my name to him suddenly, and observe how it affects him?' I accepted the trust, and am on my way to discharge it.

The sirocco has been blowing all day, and it is a hot unwholesome evening with no cool sea-breeze. Mosquitoes and fire-flies are lively enough, but most other creatures are faint. The coquettish airs of pretty young women in the tiniest and wickedest of dolls' straw hats, who lean out at opened lattice blinds, are almost the only airs stirring. Very ugly and haggard old women with distaffs, and with a grey tow upon them that looks as if they were spinning out their own hair (I suppose they were once pretty, too, but it is very difficult to believe so), sit on the footway leaning against house walls. Everybody who has come for water to the fountain, stays there, and seems incapable of any such energetic idea as going home. Vespers are over, though not so long but that I can smell the heavy resinous incense as I pass the church. No man seems to be at work, save the coppersmith. In an Italian town he is always at work, and always thumping in the deadliest manner.

I keep straight on, and come in due time to the first on the right: a narrow dull street, where I see a well-favoured man of good stature and military bearing, in a great cloak, standing at a door. Drawing nearer to this threshold, I see it is the threshold of a small wine-shop; and I can just make out, in the dim light, the inscription that it is kept by Giovanni Carlavero.

I touch my hat to the figure in the cloak, and pass in, and draw a stool to a little table. The lamp (just such another as they dig out of Pompeii) is lighted, but the place is empty. The figure in the cloak has followed me in, and stands before me.

'The Master?'

'At your service, sir.'

'Please to give me a glass of the wine of the country.'

He turns to a little counter, to get it. As his striking face is pale, and his action is evidently that of an enfeebled man, I remark that I fear he has been ill. It is not much, he courteously and gravely answers, though bad while it lasts: the fever.

As he sets the wine on the little table, to his manifest surprise I lay my hand on the back of his, look him in the face, and say in a low voice: 'I am an Englishman, and you are acquainted with a friend of mine. Do you recollect ——?' and I mentioned the name of my generous countryman.

Instantly, he utters a loud cry, bursts into tears, and falls on his knees at my feet, clasping my legs in both his arms and bowing his head to the ground.

Some years ago, this man at my feet, whose over-fraught heart is heaving as if it would burst from his breast, and whose tears are wet upon the dress I wear, was a galley-slave in the North of Italy. He was a political offender, having been concerned in the then last rising, and was sentenced to imprisonment for life. That he would have died in his chains, is certain, but for the circumstance that the Englishman happened to visit his prison.

It was one of the vile old prisons of Italy, and a part of it was below the waters of the harbour. The place of his confinement was an arched under-ground and under-water gallery, with a grill-gate at the entrance, through which it received such light and air as it got. Its condition was insufferably foul, and a stranger could hardly breathe in it, or see in it with the aid of a torch. At the upper end of this dungeon, and consequently in the worst position, as being the furthest removed from light and air, the Englishman first beheld him, sitting on an iron bedstead to which he was chained by a heavy chain. His countenance impressed the Englishman as having nothing in common with the faces of the malefactors with whom he was associated, and he talked with him, and learnt how he came to be there.

When the Englishman emerged from the dreadful den into the light of day, he asked his conductor, the governor of the jail, why Giovanni Carlavero was put into the worst place?

'Because he is particularly recommended,' was the stringent answer.

'Recommended, that is to say, for death?'

'Excuse me; particularly recommended,' was again the answer.

'He has a bad tumour in his neck, no doubt occasioned by the hardship of his miserable life. If he continues to be neglected, and he remains where he is, it will kill him.'

'Excuse me, I can do nothing. He is particularly recommended.'

The Englishman was staying in that town, and he went to his home there; but the figure of this man chained to the bedstead made it no home, and destroyed his rest and peace. He was an Englishman of an extraordinarily tender heart, and he could not bear the picture. He went back to the prison grate; went back again and again, and talked to the man and cheered him. He used the utmost influence to get the man unchained from the bedstead, were it only for ever so short a time in the day, and permitted to come to the grate. It took a long time, but the Englishman's station, personal character, and steadiness of purpose, wore out opposition so far, and that grace was at last accorded. Through the bars, when he could thus get light upon the tumour, the Englishman lanced it, and it did well and healed. His strong interest in the prisoner had greatly increased by this time, and he formed the desperate resolution that he would exert his utmost self-devotion and use his utmost efforts, to get Carlavero pardoned.

If the prisoner had been a brigand and a murderer, if he had committed every non-political crime in the Newgate Calendar and out of it, nothing would have been easier than for a man of any court or priestly influence to obtain his release. As it was, nothing could have been more difficult. Italian authorities, and English authorities who had interest with them, alike assured the Englishman that his object was hopeless. He met with nothing but evasion, refusal, and ridicule. His political prisoner became a joke in the place. It was especially observable that English Circumlocution, and English Society on its travels, were as humorous on the subject as Circumlocution and Society may be on any subject without loss of caste. But, the Englishman possessed (and proved it well in his life) a courage very uncommon among us: he had not the least fear of being considered a bore, in a good humane cause. So he went on persistently trying, and trying, and trying, to get Giovanni Carlavero out. That prisoner had been rigorously re-chained, after the tumour operation, and it was not likely that his miserable life could last very long.

One day, when all the town knew about the Englishman and his political prisoner, there came to the Englishman, a certain sprightly Italian Advocate of whom he had some knowledge; and he made this strange proposal. 'Give me a hundred pounds to obtain Carlavero's release. I think I can get him a pardon, with that money. But I cannot tell you what I am going to do with the money, nor must you ever ask me the question if I succeed, nor must you ever ask me for an account of the money if I fail.' The Englishman decided to hazard the hundred pounds. He did so, and heard not another word of the matter. For half a year and more, the Advocate made no sign, and never once 'took on' in any way, to have the subject on his mind. The Englishman was then obliged to change his residence to another and more famous town in the North of Italy. He parted from the poor prisoner with a sorrowful heart, as from a doomed man for whom there was no release but Death.

The Englishman lived in his new place of abode another half-year and more, and had no tidings of the wretched prisoner. At length, one day, he received from the Advocate a cool concise mysterious note, to this effect. 'If you still wish to bestow that benefit upon the man in whom you were once interested, send me fifty pounds more, and I think it can be ensured.' Now, the Englishman had long settled in his mind that the Advocate was a heartless sharper, who had preyed upon his credulity and his interest in an unfortunate sufferer. So, he sat down and wrote a dry answer, giving the Advocate to understand that he was wiser now than he had been formerly, and that no more money was extractable from his pocket.

He lived outside the city gates, some mile or two from the post-office, and was accustomed to walk into the city with his letters and post them himself. On a lovely spring day, when the sky was exquisitely blue, and the sea Divinely beautiful, he took his usual walk, carrying this letter to the Advocate in his pocket. As he went along, his gentle heart was much moved by the loveliness of the prospect, and by the thought of the slowly dying prisoner chained to the bedstead, for whom the universe had no delights. As he drew nearer and nearer to the city where he was to post the letter, he became very uneasy in his mind. He debated with himself, was it remotely possible, after all, that this sum of fifty pounds could restore the fellow-creature whom he pitied so much, and for whom he had striven so hard, to liberty? He was not a conventionally rich Englishman – very far from that – but, he had a spare fifty pounds at the banker's. He resolved to risk it. Without doubt, God has recompensed him for the resolution.

He went to the banker's, and got a bill for the amount, and enclosed it in a letter to the Advocate that I wish I could have seen. He simply told the Advocate that he was quite a poor man, and that he was sensible it might be a great weakness in him to part with so much money on the faith of so vague a communication; but, that there it was, and that he prayed the Advocate to make a good use of it. If he did otherwise no good could ever come of it, and it would lie heavy on his soul one day.

Within a week, the Englishman was sitting at his breakfast, when he heard some suppressed sounds of agitation on the staircase, and Giovanni Carlavero leaped into the room and fell upon his breast, a free man!

Conscious of having wronged the Advocate in his own thoughts, the Englishman wrote him an earnest and grateful letter, avowing the fact, and entreating him to confide by what means and through what agency he had succeeded so well. The Advocate returned for answer through the post, 'There are many things, as you know, in this Italy of ours, that are safest and best not even spoken of – far less written of. We may meet some day, and then I may tell you what you want to know; not here, and now.' But, the two never did meet again. The Advocate was dead when the Englishman gave me my trust; and how the man had been set free, remained as great a mystery to the Englishman, and to the man himself, as it was to me.

But, I knew this: – here was the man, this sultry night, on his knees at my feet, because I was the Englishman's friend; here were his tears upon my dress; here were his sobs choking his utterance; here were his kisses on my hands, because they had touched the hands that had worked out his release. He had no need to tell me it would be happiness to him to die for his benefactor; I doubt if I ever saw real, sterling, fervent gratitude of soul, before or since.

He was much watched and suspected, he said, and had had enough to do to keep himself out of trouble. This, and his not having prospered in his worldly affairs, had led to his having failed in his usual communications to the Englishman for – as I now remember the period – some two or three years. But, his prospects were brighter, and his wife who had been very ill had recovered, and his fever had left him, and he had bought a little vineyard, and would I carry to his benefactor the first of its wine? Ay, that I would (I told him with enthusiasm), and not a drop of it should be spilled or lost!

He had cautiously closed the door before speaking of himself, and had talked with such excess of emotion, and in a provincial Italian so difficult to understand, that I had more than once been obliged to stop him, and beg him to have compassion on me and be slower and calmer. By degrees he became so, and tranquilly walked back with me to the hotel. There, I sat down before I went to bed and wrote a faithful account of him to the Englishman: which I concluded by saying that I would bring the wine home, against any difficulties, every drop.

Early next morning, when I came out at the hotel door to pursue my journey, I found my friend waiting with one of those immense bottles in which the Italian peasants store their wine – a bottle holding some half-dozen gallons – bound round with basket-work for greater safety on the journey. I see him now, in the bright sunlight, tears of gratitude in his eyes, proudly inviting my attention to this corpulent bottle. (At the street-corner hard by, two high-flavoured able-bodied monks – pretending to talk together, but keeping their four evil eyes upon us.)

How the bottle had been got there, did not appear; but the difficulty of getting it into the ramshackle vetturino carriage in which I was departing, was so great, and it took up so much room when it was got in, that I elected to sit outside. The last I saw of Giovanni Carlavero was his running through the town by the side of the jingling wheels, clasping my hand as I stretched it down from the box, charging me with a thousand last loving and dutiful messages to his dear patron, and finally looking in at the bottle as it reposed inside, with an admiration of its honourable way of travelling that was beyond measure delightful.

And now, what disquiet of mind this dearly-beloved and highly-treasured Bottle began to cost me, no man knows. It was my precious charge through a long tour, and, for hundreds of miles, I never had it off my mind by day or by night. Over bad roads – and they were many – I clung to it with affectionate desperation. Up mountains, I looked in at it and saw it helplessly tilting over on its back, with terror. At innumerable inn doors when the weather was bad, I was obliged to be put into my vehicle before the Bottle could be got in, and was obliged to have the Bottle lifted out before human aid could come near me. The Imp of the same name, except that his associations were all evil and these associations were all good, would have been a less troublesome travelling companion. I might have served Mr Cruikshank as a subject for a new illustration of the miseries of the Bottle. The National Temperance Society might have made a powerful Tract of me.

The suspicions that attached to this innocent Bottle, greatly aggravated my difficulties. It was like the apple-pie in the child's book. Parma pouted at it, Modena mocked it, Tuscany tackled it, Naples nibbled it, Rome refused it, Austria accused it, Soldiers suspected it, Jesuits jobbed it. I composed a neat Oration, developing my inoffensive intentions in connexion with this Bottle, and delivered it in an infinity of guard-houses, at a multitude of town gates, and on every drawbridge, angle, and rampart, of a complete system of fortifications. Fifty times a day, I got down to harangue an infuriated soldiery about the Bottle. Through the filthy degradation of the abject and vile Roman

States, I had as much difficulty in working my way with the Bottle, as if it had bottled up a complete system of heretical theology. In the Neapolitan country, where everybody was a spy, a soldier, a priest, or a lazzarone, the shameless beggars of all four denominations incessantly pounced on the Bottle and made it a pretext for extorting money from me. Quires – quires do I say? Reams – of forms illegibly printed on whity-brown paper were filled up about the Bottle, and it was the subject of more stamping and sanding than I had ever seen before. In consequence of which haze of sand, perhaps, it was always irregular, and always latent with dismal penalties of going back or not going forward, which were only to be abated by the silver crossing of a base hand, poked shirtless out of a ragged uniform sleeve. Under all discouragements, however, I stuck to my Bottle, and held firm to my resolution that every drop of its contents should reach the Bottle's destination.

The latter refinement cost me a separate heap of troubles on its own separate account. What corkscrews did I see the military power bring out against that Bottle; what gimlets, spikes, divining rods, gauges, and unknown tests and instruments! At some places, they persisted in declaring that the wine must not be passed, without being opened and tasted; I, pleading to the contrary, used then to argue the question seated on the Bottle lest they should open it in spite of me. In the southern parts of Italy more violent shrieking, face-making, and gesticulating, greater vehemence of speech and countenance and action, went on about that Bottle, than would attend fifty murders in a northern latitude. It raised important functionaries out of their beds, in the dead of night. I have known half-a-dozen military lanterns to disperse themselves at all points of a great sleeping Piazza, each lantern summoning some official creature to get up, put on his cocked-hat instantly, and come and stop the Bottle. It was characteristic that while this innocent Bottle had such immense difficulty in getting from little town to town, Signor Mazzini and the fiery cross were traversing Italy from end to end.

Still, I stuck to my Bottle, like any fine old English gentleman

Devil's Bridge on the St Gotthard Road

all of the olden time. The more the Bottle was interfered with, the stauncher I became (if possible) in my first determination that my countryman should have it delivered to him intact, as the man whom he had so nobly restored to life and liberty had delivered it to me. If ever I had been obstinate in my days – and I may have been, say, once or twice – I was obstinate about the Bottle. But, I made it a rule always to keep a pocket full of small coin at its service, and never to be out of temper in its cause. Thus, I and the Bottle made our way. Once we had a break-down; rather a bad break-down, on a steep high place with the sea below us, on a tempestuous evening when it blew great guns. We were driving four wild horses abreast, Southern fashion, and there was some little difficulty in stopping them. I was outside, and not thrown off; but no words can describe my feelings when I saw the Bottle – travelling inside, as usual – burst the door open, and roll obesely out into the road. A blessed Bottle with a charmed existence, he took no hurt, and we repaired damage, and went on triumphant.

A thousand representations were made to me that the Bottle must be left at this place, or that, and called for again. I never yielded to one of them, and never parted from the Bottle, on any pretence, consideration, threat, or entreaty. I had no faith in any official receipt for the Bottle, and nothing would induce me to accept one. These unmanageable politics at last brought me and the Bottle, still triumphant, to Genoa. There, I took a tender and reluctant leave of him for a few weeks, and consigned him to a trusty English captain, to be conveyed to the Port of London by sea.

While the Bottle was on his voyage to England, I read the Shipping Intelligence as anxiously as if I had been an underwriter. There was some stormy weather after I myself had got to England by way of Switzerland and France, and my mind greatly misgave me that the Bottle might be wrecked. At last to my great joy, I received notice of his safe arrival, and immediately went down to Saint Katharine's Docks, and found him in a state of honourable captivity in the Custom House.

The wine was mere vinegar when I set it down before the

generous Englishman – probably it had been something like vinegar when I took it up from Giovanni Carlavero – but not a drop of it was spilled or gone. And the Englishman told me, with much emotion in his face and voice, that he had never tasted wine that seemed to him so sweet and sound. And long afterwards, the Bottle graced his table. And the last time I saw him in this world that misses him, he took me aside in a crowd, to say, with his amiable smile: 'We were talking of you only today at dinner, and I wished you had been there, for I had some Claret up in Carlavero's Bottle.'

A delightfully ludicrous 'Bozzy' ending to a story which, surviving all the horrors, ghastly as they are, remains in the reader's memory like a benediction.

A short note to Lord Dudley, written by Dickens from his London home in Devonshire Terrace on 28 July 1845, accompanied the triumphant delivery of the Bottle, and incidentally reveals the true name of the prisoner.

My dear Lord Dudley,

Behold Sanvanero's Bottle of Wine! His whole heart is in it, I am certain.

Faithfully yours always.

Goodbye to Italy

On 14 June Dickens left Genoa and, in a letter to Forster, he described his impressions of crossing from Italy into Switzerland.

OVER THE SAINT GOTTHARD

We came over the St Gothard, which has been open only eight days. The road is cut through the snow, and the carriage winds along a narrow path between two massive snow walls, twenty feet high or more. Vast plains of snow range up the mountain-sides above the road, itself seven thousand feet above the sea; and tremendous waterfalls, hewing out arches for themselves in the vast drifts, go thundering down from precipices into deep chasms, here and there and everywhere; the blue water tearing through the white snow with an awful beauty that is most sublime. The pass itself, the mere pass over the top, is not so fine, I think, as the Simplon; and there is no plain upon the summit, for the moment it is reached the descent begins. So that the loneliness and wildness of the Simplon are not equalled *there*. But being much higher, the ascent and the descent range over a much greater space of country; and on both sides there are places of terrible grandeur, unsurpassable, I should imagine, in the world. The Devil's Bridge, terrific! The whole descent between Andermatt (where we slept on Friday night) and Altdorf, William Tell's town, which we passed through yesterday afternoon, is the highest sublimation of all you can imagine in the way of Swiss scenery. Oh God! what a beautiful country it is! How poor and sunken, beside it, is Italy in its brightest aspect!

I look upon the coming down from the Great St Gothard with a carriage and four horses and only one postilion, as the most dangerous thing that a carriage and horses can do. We had two great wooden logs for drags, and snapped them both like matches. The road is like a geometrical staircase, with horrible depths beneath it; and at every turn it is a toss-up, or seems to be, whether the leaders shall go round or over. The lives of the whole party may depend upon a strap in the harness; and if we broke our rotten harness once yesterday, we broke it at least a dozen times. The difficulty of keeping the horses together in the continual and steep circle, is immense. They slip and slide, and get their legs over the traces, and are dragged up against the rocks; carriage, horses, harness, all a confused heap. The Brave, and I, and the postilion, were constantly at work, in extricating the whole concern from a tangle, like a skein of thread. We broke two thick iron chains, and crushed the box of a wheel, as it was; and the carriage is now undergoing repair, under the window, on the margin of the lake: where a woman in short petticoats, a stomacher, and two immensely long tails of black hair hanging down her back very nearly to her heels, is looking on – apparently dressed for a melodrama, but in reality a waitress at this establishment.

If the Swiss villages looked beautiful to me in winter, their summer aspect is most charming: most fascinating: most delicious. Shut in by high mountains capped with perpetual snow; and dotting a rich carpet of the softest turf, overshadowed by great trees; they seem so many little havens of refuge from the troubles and miseries of great towns. The cleanliness of the little baby-houses of inns is wonderful to those who come from Italy. But the beautiful Italian manners, the sweet language, the quick recognition of a pleasant look or cheerful word; the captivating expression of a desire to oblige in everything; are left behind the Alps. Remembering them, I sigh for the dirt again: the brick floors, bare walls, unplastered ceilings, and broken windows.

In Switzerland

Dickens remained in England for a year. During the spring of 1846 he edited for a short time his new radical paper, The Daily News, *in which six of his Italian letters appeared. Forster succeeded him as editor and, in May, the completed* Pictures from Italy *with illustrations by Samuel Palmer was published in book form.*

In June, with Roche again as man-of-all-parts, he and the family set out once more in the lumbering coach across France to Switzerland. The most memorable account of this new journey, 'Travelling Abroad', was written years later by 'The Uncommercial' (as he called himself) and, like 'The Calais Night Mail', is a kaleidoscopic fusion of past and present. The traveller takes up into his lumbering dream-coach that very child 'abroad in the world with his eyes open' who at the age of nine had fallen inescapably in love with the house called Gadshill Place, where now, the impossible actually realised, the child who had become the most famous novelist in the world was spending the last years of his life.

TRAVELLING ABROAD

I got into the travelling chariot – it was of German make, roomy, heavy, and unvarnished – I got into the travelling chariot, pulled up the steps after me, shut myself in with a smart bang of the door, and gave the word, 'Go on!'

Immediately, all that W. and S.W. division of London began to slide away at a pace so lively, that I was over the river, and past the Old Kent Road, and out on Blackheath, and even ascending Shooter's Hill, before I had had time to look about me in the carriage, like a collected traveller.

I had two ample Imperials on the roof, other fitted storage for luggage in front, and other up behind; I had a net for books overhead, great pockets to all the windows, a leathern pouch or two hung up for odds and ends, and a reading lamp fixed in the back of the chariot, in case I should be benighted. I was amply provided in all respects, and had no idea where I was going (which was delightful), except that I was going abroad.

So smooth was the old high road, and so fresh were the horses, and so fast went I, that it was midway between Gravesend and Rochester, and the widening river was bearing the ships, white-sailed or black-smoked, out to sea, when I noticed by the wayside a very queer small boy.

'Hoalloa!' said I, to the very queer small boy, 'where do you live?'

'At Chatham' says he.

'What do you do there?' says I.

'I go to school,' says he.

I took him up in a moment, and we went on. Presently, the very queer small boy says, 'This is Gads-hill we are coming to, where Falstaff went out to rob those travellers, and ran away.'

'You know something about Falstaff, eh?' said I.

'All about him,' said the very queer small boy. 'I am old (I am nine), and I read all sorts of books. But *do* let us stop at the top of the hill, and look at the house there, if you please!'

'You admire that house?' said I.

'Bless you, sir,' said the very queer small boy, 'when I was not more than half as old as nine, it used to be a treat for me to be brought to look at it. And now, I am nine, I come by myself to look at it. And ever since I can recollect, my father, seeing me so fond of it, has often said to me, "If you were to be very persevering and were to work hard, you might some day come to live in it." Though that's impossible!' said the very queer small boy, drawing a low breath, and now staring at the house out of window with all his might.

I was rather amazed to be told this by the very queer small boy; for that house happens to be *my* house, and I have reason to believe that what he said was true.

Well! I made no halt there, and I soon dropped the very queer small boy and went on. Over the road where the old Romans used to march, over the road where the old Canterbury pilgrims used to go, over the road where the travelling trains of the old imperious priests and princes used to jingle on horseback between the continent and this Island through the mud and water, over the road where Shakespeare hummed to himself, 'Blow, blow, thou winter wind,' as he sat in the saddle at the gate of the inn yard noticing the carriers; all among the cherry orchards, apple orchards, corn-fields, and hop-gardens; so went I, by Canterbury to Dover. There, the sea was tumbling in, with deep sounds, after dark, and the revolving French light on Cape Grinez was seen regularly bursting out and becoming obscured, as if the head of a gigantic light-keeper in an anxious state of mind were interposed every half-minute, to look how it was burning.

Early in the morning I was on the deck of the steam-packet, and we were aiming at the bar in the usual intolerable manner, and the bar was aiming at us in the usual intolerable manner, and the bar got by far the best of it, and we got by far the worst – all in the usual intolerable manner.

But, when I was clear of the Custom House on the other side, and when I began to make the dust fly on the thirsty French roads, and when the twigsome trees by the wayside (which, I suppose, never will grow leafy, for they never did) guarded here and there a dusty soldier, or field labourer, baking on a heap of broken stones, sound asleep in a fiction of shade, I began to recover my travelling spirits. Coming upon the breaker of the broken stones, in a hard hot shining hat, on which the sun played at a distance as on a burning-glass, I felt that now, indeed, I was in the dear old France of my affections. I should have known it, without the well-remembered bottle of rough ordinary wine, the cold roast fowl, the loaf, and the pinch of salt, on which I lunched with unspeakable satisfaction, from one of the stuffed pockets of the chariot.

I must have fallen asleep after lunch, for when a bright face looked in at the window, I started, and said:

'Good God, Louis, I dreamed you were dead!'

My cheerful servant laughed, and answered:
'Me? Not at all, sir.'
'How glad I am to wake! What are we doing, Louis?'
'We go to take relay of horses. Will you walk up the hill?'
'Certainly.'

Welcome the old French hill, with the old French lunatic (not in the most distant degree related to Sterne's Maria) living in a thatched dog-kennel half-way up, and flying out with his crutch and his big head and extended nightcap, to be beforehand with the old men and women exhibiting crippled children, and with the children exhibiting old men and women, ugly and blind, who always seemed by resurrectionary process to be recalled out of the elements for the sudden peopling of the solitude!'

'It is well,' said I, scattering among them what small coin I had; 'here comes Louis, and I am quite roused from my nap.'

We journeyed on again, and I welcomed every new assurance that France stood where I had left it. There were the posting-houses, with their archways, dirty stable-yards, and clean post-masters' wives, bright women of business, looking on at the putting-to of the horses; there were the postilions counting what money they got, into their hats, and never making enough of it; there were the standard population of grey horses of Flanders descent, invariably biting one another when they got a chance; there were the fleecy sheepskins, looped on over their uniforms by the postilions, like bibbed aprons when it blew and rained; there were their jackboots, and their cracking whips; there were the cathedrals that I got out to see, as under some cruel bondage, in no wise desiring to see them; there were the little towns that appeared to have no reason for being towns, since most of their houses were to let and nobody could be induced to look at them, except the people who couldn't let them and had nothing else to do but look at them all day. I lay a night upon the road and enjoyed delectable cookery of potatoes, and some other sensible things, adoption of which at home would inevitably be shown to be fraught with ruin, somehow or other, to that rickety national blessing, the British farmer; and at last I was rattled, like a single pill in a box, over leagues of stones, until – madly cracking, plunging, and flourishing two grey tails about – I made my triumphal entry into Paris.

At Paris, I took an upper apartment for a few days in one of the hotels of the Rue de Rivoli; my front windows looking into the garden of the Tuileries (where the principal difference between the nursemaids and the flowers seemed to be that the former were locomotive and the latter not): my back windows looking at all the other back windows in the hotel, and deep down into a paved yard, where my German chariot had retired under a tight-fitting archway, to all appearance for life, and where bells rang all day without anybody's minding them but certain chamberlains with feather brooms and green baize caps, who here and there leaned out of some high window placidly looking down, and where neat waiters with trays on their left shoulders passed and repassed from morning to night.

Whenever I am at Paris, I am dragged by invisible force into the Morgue. I never want to go there, but am always pulled there. One Christmas Day, when I would rather have been anywhere else, I was attracted in, to see an old grey man lying all alone on his cold bed, with a tap of water turned on over his grey hair, and running, drip, drip, drip, down his wretched face until it got to the corner of his mouth, where it took a turn, and made him look sly. One New Year's Morning (by the same token, the sun was shining outside, and there was a mountebank balancing a feather on his nose, within a yard of the gate), I was pulled in again to look at a flaxen-haired boy of eighteen, with a heart hanging on his breast – 'from his mother,' was engraven on it – who had come into the net across the river, with a bullet wound in his fair forehead and his hands cut with a knife, but whence or how was a blank mystery. This time, I was forced into the same dread place, to see a large dark man whose disfigurement by water was in a frightful manner comic, and whose expression was that of a prize-fighter who had closed his eyelids under a heavy blow, but was going immediately to open them, shake his head, and 'come up smiling'. Oh what this large dark man cost me in that bright city!

It was very hot weather, and he was none the better for that, and I was much the worse. Indeed, a very neat and pleasant little woman with the key of her lodging on her forefinger, who had been showing him to her little girl while she and the child ate sweetmeats, observed monsieur looking poorly as we came out together, and asked monsieur, with her wondering little eyebrows prettily raised, if there were anything the matter? Faintly replying in the negative, monsieur crossed the road to a wine-shop, got some brandy, and resolved to freshen himself with a dip in the great floating bath on the river.

The bath was crowed in the usual airy manner, by a male population in striped drawers of various gay colours, who walked up and down arm in arm, drank coffee, smoked cigars, sat at little tables, conversed politely with the damsels who dispensed the towels, and every now and then pitched themselves into the river head foremost, and came out again to repeat this social routine. I made haste to participate in the water part of the entertainments, and was in the full enjoyment of a delightful bath, when all in a moment I was seized with an unreasonable idea that the large dark body was floating straight at me.

I was out of the river, and dressing instantly. In the shock I had taken some water into my mouth, and it turned me sick, for I fancied that the contamination of the creature was in it. I had got back to my cool darkened room in the hotel, and was lying on a sofa there, before I began to reason with myself.

Of course, I knew perfectly well that the large dark creature was stone dead, and that I should no more come upon him out of the place where I had seen him dead, than I should come upon the cathedral of Notre-Dame in an entirely new situation. What troubled me was the picture of the creature; and that had so curiously and strongly painted itself upon my brain, that I could not get rid of it until it was worn out.

I noticed the peculiarities of this possession, while it was a real discomfort to me. That very day, at dinner, some morsel on my plate looked like a piece of him, and I was glad to get up and go out. Later in the evening, I was walking along the Rue St Honore, when I saw a bill at a public room there, announcing small-sword exercise, broadsword exercise, wrestling, and other such feats. I went in, and some of the sword-play being very skilful, remained. A specimen of our own national sport, The British Boaxe, was announced to be given at the close of the evening. In an evil hour, I determined to wait for this Boaxe, as became a Briton. It was a clumsy specimen (executed by two English grooms out of place), but one of the combatants, receiving a straight right-hander with the glove between his eyes, did exactly what the large dark creature in the Morgue had seemed going to do – and finished me for that night.

There was rather a sickly smell (not at all an unusual fragrance in Paris) in the little ante-room of my apartment at the hotel. The large dark creature in the Morgue was by no direct experience associated with my sense of smell, because, when I came to the knowledge of him, he lay behind a wall of thick plate-glass as good as a wall of steel or marble for that matter. Yet the whiff of the room never failed to reproduce him. What was more curious, was the capriciousness with which his portrait seemed to light itself up in my mind, elsewhere. I might be walking in the Palais Royal, lazily enjoying the shop windows, and might be regaling myself with one of the ready-made clothes shops that are set out there. My eyes, wandering over impossible-waisted dressing-gowns and luminous waistcoats, would fall upon the master, or the shopman, or even the very dummy at the door, and would suggest to me, 'Something like him!' – and instantly I was sickened again.

This would happen at the theatre, in the same manner. Often it would happen in the street, when I certainly was not looking for the likeness, and when probably there was no likeness there. It was not because the creature was dead that I was so haunted, because I know that I might have been (and I know it because I have been) equally attended by the image of a living aversion. This lasted about a week. The picture did not fade by degrees, in the sense that it became a whit less forcible and distinct, but in the sense that it obtruded itself less and less frequently. The experience may be worth considering by some who have the care of children. It would be difficult to overstate the intensity and accuracy of an intelligent child's observation. At that impressible time of life, it must sometimes produce a fixed impression. If the fixed impression be of an object terrible to the child, it will be (for want of reasoning upon) inseparable from great fear. Force the child at such a time, be Spartan with it, send it into the dark against its will, leave it in a lonely bedroom against its will, and you had better murder it.

On a bright morning I rattled away from Paris, in the German chariot, and left the large dark creature behind me for good. I ought to confess, though, that I had been drawn back to the Morgue, after he was put underground, to look at his clothes, and that I found them frightfully like him – particularly his boots. However, I rattled away for Switzerland, looking forward and not backward, and so we parted company.

Welcome again, the long long spell of France, with the queer country inns, full of vases of flowers and clocks, in the dull little town, and with the little population not at all dull on the little Boulevard in the evening, under the little trees! Welcome Monsieur the Curé, walking alone in the early morning a short way out of the town, reading that eternal Breviary of yours, which surely might be almost read, without book, by this time! Welcome Monsieur the Curé, later in the day, jolting through the highway dust (as if you had already ascended to the cloudy region), in a very big-headed cabriolet, with the dried mud of a dozen winters on it. Welcome again Monsieur the Curé, as we exchange salutations; you, straightening your back to look at the German chariot, while picking in your little village garden a vegetable or two for the day's soup: I, looking out of the German chariot window in that delicious traveller's trance which knows no cares, no yesterdays, no to-morrows, nothing but the passing objects and the passing scents and sounds! And so I came, in due course of delight, to Strasbourg, where I passed a wet Sunday evening at a window, while an idle trifle of a vaudeville was played for me at the opposite house.

How such a large house came to have only three people living in it, was its own affair. There were at least a score of windows in its high roof alone; how many in its grotesque front, I soon gave up counting. The owner was a shopkeeper, by name Straudenheim; by trade – I couldn't make out what by trade, for he had forborne to write that up, and his shop was shut.

At first, as I looked at Straudenheim's, through the steadily falling rain, I set him up in business in the goose-liver line. But, inspection of Straudenheim, who became visible at a window on the second floor, convinced me that there was something more precious than liver in the case. He wore a black velvet skull-cap, and looked usurious and rich. A large-lipped, pear-nosed old man, with white hair, and keen eyes, though near-sighted. He was writing at a desk, was Straudenheim, and ever and again left off writing, put his pen in his mouth, and went through actions with his right hand, like a man steadying piles of cash. Five-franc pieces, Straudenheim, or golden Napoleons? A jeweller, Straudenheim, a dealer in money, a diamond merchant, or what?

Below Straudenheim, at a window on the first floor, sat his housekeeper – far from young, but of a comely presence, suggestive of a well-matured foot and ankle. She was cheerily dressed, had a fan in her hand, and wore large gold earrings and a large gold cross. She would have been out holiday-making (as I settled it) but for the pestilent rain. Strasbourg had given up holiday-making for that once, as a bad job, because the rain was jerking in gushes out of the old roof-spouts, and running in a brook down the middle of the street. The housekeeper, her arms folded on her bosom and her fan tapping her chin, was bright and smiling at her open window, but otherwise Straudenheim's house front was very dreary. The housekeeper's was the only open window in it; Straudenheim kept himself close, though it was a sultry evening when air is pleasant, and though the rain had brought into the town that vague refreshing smell of grass which rain does bring in the summer-time.

The dim appearance of a man at Straudenheim's shoulder, inspired me with a misgiving that somebody had come to murder that flourishing merchant for the wealth with which I had handsomely endowed him: the rather, as it was an excited man, lean and long of figure, and evidently stealthy of foot. But, he conferred with Straudenheim instead of doing him a mortal injury, and then they both softly opened the other window of that room

– which was immediately over the housekeeper's – and tried to see her by looking down. And my opinion of Straudenheim was much lowered when I saw that eminent citizen spit out of window, clearly with the hope of spitting on the housekeeper.

The unconscious housekeeper fanned herself, tossed her head, and laughed. Though unconscious of Straudenheim, she was conscious of somebody else – of me? – there was nobody else.

After leaning so far out of the window, that I confidently expected to see their heels tilt up, Straudenheim and the lean man drew their heads in and shut the window. Presently, the house door secretly opened, and they slowly and spitefully crept forth into the pouring rain. They were coming over to me (I thought) to demand satisfaction for my looking at the housekeeper, when they plunged into a recess in the architecture under my window and dragged out the puniest of little soldiers, begirt with the most innocent of little swords. The tall glazed head-dress of this warrior, Straudenheim instantly knocked off, and out of it fell two sugar-sticks, and three or four large lumps of sugar.

The warrior made no effort to recover his property or to pick up his shako, but looked with an expression of attention at Straudenheim when he kicked him five times, and also at the lean man when *he* kicked him five times, and again at Straudenheim when he tore the breast of his (the warrior's) little coat open, and shook all his ten fingers in his face, as if they were ten thousand. When these outrages had been committed, Straudenheim and his man went into the house again and barred the door. A wonderful circumstance was, that the housekeeper who saw it all (and who could have taken six such warriors to her buxom bosom at once), only fanned herself and laughed as she had laughed before, and seemed to have no opinion about it, one way or other.

But, the chief effect of the drama was the remarkable vengeance taken by the little warrior. Left alone in the rain, he picked up his shako; put it on, all wet and dirty as it was; retired into a court, of which Straudenheim's house formed the corner; wheeled about; and bringing his two forefingers close to the top of his nose, rubbed them over one another, cross-wise, in derision, defiance, and contempt of Straudenheim. Although Straudenheim could not possibly be supposed to be conscious of this strange proceeding, it so inflated and comforted the little warrior's soul, that twice he went away, and twice came back into the court to repeat it, as though it must goad his enemy to madness. Not only that, but he afterwards came back with two other small warriors, and they all three did it together. Not only that – as I live to tell the tale! – but just as it was falling quite dark, the three came back, bringing with them a huge bearded Sapper, whom they moved, by recital of the original wrong, to go through the same performance, with the same complete absence of all possible knowledge of it on the part of Straudenheim. And then they all went away, arm in arm, singing.

I went away too, in the German chariot at sunrise, and rattled on, day after day, like one in a sweet dream; with so many clear little bells on the harness of the horses, that the nursery rhyme about Banbury Cross and the venerable lady who rode in state there, was always in my ears. And now I came to the land of wooden houses, innocent cakes, thin butter soup, and spotless little inn bedrooms with a family likeness to Dairies. And now the Swiss marksmen were for ever rifle-shooting at marks across gorges, so exceedingly near my ear, that I felt like a new Gesler in a Canton of Tells, and went in highly-deserved danger of my tyrannical life. The prizes at these shootings, were watches, smart handkerchiefs, hats, spoons, and (above all) tea-trays; and at these contests I came upon a more than usually accomplished and amiable countryman of my own, who had shot himself deaf in whole years of competition, and had won so many tea-trays that he went about the country with his carriage full of them, like a glorified Cheap-Jack.

In the mountain-country into which I had now travelled, a yoke of oxen were sometimes hooked on before the post-horses, and I went lumbering up, up, up, through mist and rain, with the roar of falling water for change of music. Of a sudden, mist and rain would clear away, and I would come down into picturesque little towns with gleaming spires and odd towers; and would stroll afoot into market-places in steep winding streets, where a hundred women in bodices, sold eggs and honey, butter and fruit, and suckled their children as they sat by their clean baskets, and had such enormous goîtres (or glandular swellings in the throat) that it became a science to know where the nurse ended and the child began. About this time, I deserted my German chariot for the back of a mule (in colour and consistency so very like a dusty old hair trunk I once had at school, that I half expected to see my initials in brass-headed nails on his backbone), and went up a thousand rugged ways, and looked down at a thousand woods of fir and pine, and would on the whole have preferred my mule's keeping a little nearer to the inside, and not usually travelling with a hoof or two over the precipice – though much consoled by explanation that this was to be attributed to his great sagacity, by reason of his carrying broad loads of wood at other times, and not being clear but that I myself belonged to that station of life, and required as much room as they. He brought me safely, in his own wise way, among the passes of the Alps, and here I enjoyed a dozen climates a day; being now (like Don Quixote on the back of the wooden horse) in the region of wind, now in the region of fire, now in the region of unmelting ice and snow. Here, I passed over trembling domes of ice, beneath which the cataract was roaring; and here was received under arches of icicles, of unspeakable beauty; and here the sweet air was so bracing and so light, that at halting-times I rolled in the snow when I saw my mule do it, thinking that he must know best. At this part of the journey we would come, at mid-day, into half an hour's thaw: when the rough mountain inn would be found on an island of deep mud in a sea of snow, while the baiting strings of mules, and the carts full of casks and bales, which had been in an Arctic condition a mile off, would steam again. By such ways and means, I would come to the cluster of châlets where I had to turn out of the track to see the waterfall; and then, uttering a howl like a young giant, on espying a traveller – in other words, something to eat – coming up the steep, the idiot lying on the wood-pile who sunned himself and nursed his goître, would rouse the woman-guide within the hut, who would

Rosemont Villa, Lausanne, August 1846

stream out hastily, throwing her child over one of her shoulders and her goître over the other, as she came along. I slept at religious houses, and bleak refuges of many kinds, on this journey, and by the stove at night heard stories of travellers who had perished within call, in wreaths and drifts of snow. One night the stove within, and the cold outside, awakened childish associations long forgotten, and I dreamed I was in Russia – the identical serf out of a picture-book I had, before I could read it for myself – and that I was going to be knouted by a noble personage in a fur cap, boots, and earrings, who, I think, must have come out of some melodrama.

Commend me to the beautiful waters among these mountains! Though I was not of their mind: they, being inveterately bent on getting down into the level country, and I ardently desiring to linger where I was. What desperate leaps they took, what dark abysses they plunged into, what rocks they wore away, what echoes they invoked! In one part where I went, they were pressed into the service of carrying wood down, to be burnt next winter, as costly fuel, in Italy. But, their fierce savage nature was not to be easily constrained, and they fought with every limb of the wood; whirling it round and round, stripping its bark away, dashing it against pointed corners, driving it out of the course, and roaring and flying at the peasants who steered it back again from the bank with long stout poles. Alas! concurrent streams of time and water carried *me* down fast, and I came, on an exquisitely clear day, to the Lausanne shore of the Lake of Geneva, where I stood looking at the bright blue water, the flushed white mountains opposite, and the boats at my feet with their furled Mediterranean sails, showing like enormous magnifications of this goose-quill pen that is now in my hand.

– The sky became overcast without any notice; a wind very like the March east wind of England, blew across me; and a voice said, 'How do you like it? Will it do?'

I had merely shut myself, for half a minute, in a German travelling chariot that stood for sale in the Carriage Department of the London Pantechnicon. I had a commission to buy it, for a friend who was going abroad; and the look and manner of the chariot, as I tried the cushions and the springs, brought all these hints of travelling remembrance before me.

'It will do very well,' said I, rather sorrowfully, as I got out at the other door, and shut the carriage up.

In Lausanne Dickens found 'quite a little dolls' house' – 'Rosemont' – and, in two letters of mid-June, he sent Forster a description both of it and of the surrounding countryside.

'ROSEMONT'

It is beautifully situated on the hill that rises from the lake, within ten minutes' walk of this hotel, and furnished, though scantily as all here are, better than others except Elysée, on account of its having been built and fitted up (the little *salons* in the Parisian way) by the landlady and her husband for themselves. They live now in a smaller house like a porter's lodge, just within the gate. A portion of the grounds is farmed by a farmer, and *he* lives close by; so that, while it is secluded, it is not at all lonely . . .

My little study is upstairs, and looks out, from two French windows opening into a balcony, on the lake and mountains; and that there are roses enough to smother the whole establishment of the *Daily News* in. Likewise, there is a pavilion in the garden, which has but two rooms in it; in one of which I think you shall do your work when you come. As to bowers for reading and smoking, there are as many scattered about the grounds as there are in Chalk Farm tea-gardens. But the Rosemont bowers are really beautiful. Will you come to the bowers . . ?

The country is delightful in the extreme – as leafy, green, and shady, as England; full of deep glens, and branchy places (rather a Leigh Huntish expression), and bright with all sorts of flowers in profusion. It abounds in singing birds besides – very pleasant after Italy; and the moonlight on the lake is noble. Prodigious mountains rise up from its opposite shore (it is eight or nine miles across, at this point), and the Simplon, the St Gothard, Mont Blanc and all the Alpine wonders are piled there, in tremendous grandeur. The cultivation is uncommonly rich and profuse. There are all manner of walks, vineyard, green lanes, cornfields, and pastures full of hay. The general neatness is as remarkable as in England. There are no priests or monks in the streets, and the people appear to be industrious and thriving. French (and very intelligible and pleasant French) seems to be the universal language. I never saw so many booksellers' shops crammed within the same space, as in the steep up-and-down streets of Lausanne.

There are some suppressed churches in it, now used as packers' warehouses: with cranes and pulleys growing out of steeple-towers; little doors for lowering goods through, fitted into blocked-up oriel windows; and cart-horses stabled in crypts. These also help it to give a deserted and disused appearance. On the other hand, as it is a perfectly free place subject to no prohibitions or restrictions of any kind, there are all sorts of new French books and publications in it, and all sorts of fresh intelligence from the world beyond the Jura Mountains. It contains only one Roman Catholic church, which is mainly for the use of the Savoyards and Piedmontese who come trading over the Alps. As for the country, it cannot be praised too highly, or reported too beautiful. There are no great waterfalls, or walks through mountain-gorges, *close* at hand, as in some other parts of Switzerland; but there is a charming variety of enchanting scenery. There is the shore of the lake, where you may dip your feet, as you walk, in the deep blue water, if you choose. There are the hills to climb up, leading to the great heights above the town; or to stagger down, leading to the lake. There is every possible variety of deep green lanes, vineyard, cornfield, pasture-land, and wood. There are excellent country roads that might be in Kent or Devonshire; and, closing up every view and vista, is an eternally changing range of prodigious mountains – sometimes red, sometimes grey, sometimes purple, sometimes black, sometimes white with snow; sometimes close at hand; and sometimes very ghosts in the clouds and mist.

Dickens, however, did not remain all the time in Lausanne, and two of the trips he made further afield he described in his letters to Forster.

CROSSING THE COL DE BALME

I begin my letter to-night, but only begin, for we returned from Chamonix in time for dinner just now, and are pretty considerably done up. We went by a mountain pass not often crossed by ladies, called the Col de Balme, where your imagination may picture Kate and Georgy on mules *for ten hours at a stretch* riding up and down the most frightful precipices. We returned by the pass of the Tête Noire, which Talfourd knows, and which is of a different character, but astonishingly fine too. Mont Blanc, and the Valley of Chamonix, and the Mer de Glace, and all the wonders of that most wonderful place, are above and beyond one's wildest expectations. I cannot imagine anything in nature more stupendous or sublime. If I were to write about it now, I should quite rave – such prodigious impressions are rampant within me. . . . You may suppose that the mule-travelling is pretty primitive. Each person takes a carpet-bag strapped on the mule behind himself or herself: and that is all the baggage that can be carried. A guide, a thorough-bred mountaineer, walks all the way, leading the lady's mule; I say lady's *par excellence*, in compliment to Kate; and all the rest struggle on as they please. The cavalcade stops at a lone hut for an hour and a half in the middle of the day, and lunches brilliantly on whatever it can get. Going by that Col de Balme pass, you climb up and up and up for five hours and more, and look – from a mere unguarded ledge of path on the side of the precipice – into such awful valleys, that at last you are firm in the belief that you have got above everything in the world, and that there can be nothing earthly overhead. Just as you arrive at this conclusion, a different (and O! Heaven! what a free and wonderful) air comes blowing on your face; you cross a ridge of snow; and lying before you (wholly unseen till then), towering up into the distant sky, is the vast range of Mont Blanc, with attendant mountains diminished by its majestic side into mere dwarfs tapering up into innumerable rude Gothic pinnacles; deserts of ice and snow; forests of firs on mountain sides, of no account at all in the enormous scene; villages down in the hollow, that you can shut out with a finger; waterfalls, avalanches, pyramids and towers of ice, torrents, bridges; mountain upon mountain until the very sky is blocked away, and you must look up, overhead, to see it. Good God, what a country Switzerland is, and what a concentration of it is to be beheld from that one spot! And (think of this in Whitefriars and in Lincoln's Inn!) at noon on the second day from here, the first day being but half a one by the by and full of uncommon beauty, you lie down on that ridge and see it all! . . . I think I must go back again (whether you come or not!) and see it again before the bad weather arrives. We have had sunlight, moonlight, a perfectly transparent atmosphere with not a cloud, and the grand plateau on the very summit of Mont Blanc so clear by day and night that it was difficult to believe in intervening chasms and precipices, and almost impossible to resist the idea that one might sally forth and climb up easily. I went into all sorts of places; armed with a great pole with a spike at the end of it, like a leaping-pole, and with pointed irons buckled on to my shoes; and am all but knocked up. I was very anxious to make the expedition to what is called 'The Garden': a green spot covered with wild flowers, lying across the Mer de Glace, and among the most awful mountains: but I could find no Englishman at the hotels who was similarly disposed, and the Brave *wouldn't* go. No, sir! He gave in point blank (having been horribly blown in a climbing excursion the day before), and couldn't stand it. He is too heavy for such work, unquestionably. In all other respects, I think he has exceeded himself on this journey: and if you could have seen him riding a very small mule up a road exactly like the broken stairs of Rochester Castle, with a brandy bottle slung over his shoulder, a small pie in his hat, a roast fowl looking out of his pocket, and a mountain staff of six feet long carried crosswise on the saddle before him, you'd have said so. He was (next to me) the admiration of Chamonix, but he utterly quenched me on the road.

THE GREAT SAINT BERNARD

The weather obstinately clearing, we started off last Tuesday for the Great St Bernard, returning here on Friday afternoon. The party consisted of eleven people and two servants – Haldimand, Mr and Mrs Cerjat and one daughter, Mr and Mrs Watson, two Ladies Taylor, Kate, Georgy, and I. We were wonderfully unanimous and cheerful; went away from here by the steamer; found at its destination a whole omnibus provided by the Brave (who went on in advance everywhere); rode therein to Bex; found two large carriages ready to take us to Martigny; slept there; and proceeded up the mountain on mules next day. Although the St Bernard convent is, as I dare say you know, the highest inhabited spot but one in the world, the ascent is extremely gradual and uncommonly easy: really presenting no difficulties at all, until within the last league, when the ascent, lying through a place called the valley of desolation, is very awful and tremendous, and the road is rendered toilsome by scattered rocks and melting snow. The convent is a most extraordinary place, full of great vaulted passages, divided from each other with iron gratings; and presenting a series of the most astonishing little dormitories, where the windows are so small (on account of the cold and snow), that it is as much as one can do to get one's head out of them. Here we slept: supping, thirty strong, in a rambling room with a great wood-fire in it set apart for that purpose; with a grim monk, in a high black sugar-loaf hat with a great knob at the top of it, carving the dishes. At five o'clock in the morning the chapel bell rang in the dismallest way for matins: and I, lying in bed close to the chapel, and being awakened by the solemn organ and the chaunting, thought for a moment I had died in the night and passed into the unknown world.

I wish to God you could see that place. A great hollow on the top of a range of dreadful mountains, fenced in by riven rocks of every shape and colour: and in the midst, a black lake, with phantom clouds perpetually stalking over it. Peaks, and points, and plains of eternal ice and snow, bounding the view, and shutting out the world on every side: the lake reflecting nothing: and no human figure in the scene. The air so fine, that it is difficult to breathe without feeling out of breath; and the cold so exquisitely thin and sharp that it is not to be described. Nothing of life or living interest in the picture, but the grey dull walls of the convent. No vegetation of any sort or kind. Nothing growing, nothing stirring. Everything iron-bound, and frozen up. Beside the convent, in a little outhouse with a grated iron door which you may unbolt for yourself, are the bodies of people found in the snow who have never been claimed and are withering away – not laid down, or stretched out, but standing up, in corners and against walls; some erect and horribly human, with distinct expressions on the faces; some sunk down on their knees; some dropping over on one side; some tumbled down altogether, and presenting a heap of skulls and fibrous dust. There is no other decay in that atmosphere; and there they remain during the short days and the long nights, the only human company out of doors, withering away by grains, and holding ghastly possession of the mountain where they died.

It is the most distinct and individual place I have seen, even in this transcendent country. But, for the Saint Bernard holy fathers and convent in themselves, I am sorry to say that they are a piece of as sheer humbug as we ever learnt to believe in, in our young days. Trashy French sentiment and the dogs (of which, by the bye, there are only three remaining) have done it all. They are a lazy set of fellows; not over fond of going out themselves; employing servants to clear the road (which has not been important or much used as a pass these hundred years); rich; and driving a good trade in Innkeeping: the convent being a common tavern in everything but the sign. No charge is made for their hospitality, to be sure; but you are shown to a box in the chapel, where everybody puts in more than could, with any show of face, be charged for the entertainment; and from this the establishment derives a right good income. As to the self-sacrifice of living up there, they are obliged to go there young, it is true, to be inured to the climate: but it is an infinitely more exciting and various life than any other convent can offer; with constant change and company through the whole summer; with a hospital for invalids down in the valley, which affords another change; and with an annual begging-journey to Geneva and this place and all the places round for one brother or other, which affords further change. The brother who carved at our supper could speak some

English, and had just had *Pickwick* given him! – what a humbug he will think me when he tries to understand it! If I had any other book of mine with me, I would have given it him, that I might have had some chance of being intelligible.

But writing was still his main concern and, happily settled in 'Rosemont', Dickens waited for the arrival of his box of writing materials and his favourite little ornaments, including two fighting frogs which, because of some strange magical power to set him writing, he always felt he must *have on his desk.*

WRITING IN LAUSANNE

When his box came, Dickens turned his mind to the new novel over which he had been brooding for some time. And during the walks in the Swiss countryside with which he varied the sessions at his desk, an idea had come to him for his next Christmas book. 'An odd shadowy, unidentified idea is at work within me that I could connect a great battlefield somehow with my Christmas story . . . Shapeless visions of the repose and peace pervading it in after time, with the corn and grass growing over the slain, and people singing at the plough.' So the story with which he was to struggle side by side with his novel was called 'The Battle of Life' – apart from its striking opening, the least satisfactory of all his Christmas Books. *But soon he was to write triumphantly to Forster*:

BEGAN DOMBEY. I performed this feat yesterday – only wrote the first slip – but there it is and a plunge straight over head and ears into the story . . . Besides all this, I have really gone with great vigour at the French, where I find myself greatly assisted by the Italian . . .

By the way, as I was unpacking the big box I took hold of a book and said to 'Them', 'Now, whatever passage my thumb rests on, I shall take as having reference to my work'.

The book was Tristram Shandy, *and it opened at these words: 'What a work it is likely to turn out. Let us begin it.' But, whatever the ultimate success of* Dombey, *Dickens revealed to Forster, in a passage which has become famous, that at this period his work was being hindered by an obsessive craving which had always haunted him when he became deeply involved in creative writing.*

You can hardly imagine what infinite pains I take, or what extraordinary difficulty I find in getting on FAST. Invention, thank God, seems the easiest thing in the world; and I seem to have such a preposterous sense of the ridiculous after this long rest, as to be constantly restraining myself from launching into extravagances in the height of my enjoyment. But the difficulty of going at what I call a rapid pace, is prodigious; it is almost an impossibility. I suppose this is partly the effect of two years' ease, and partly of the absence of streets and numbers of figures. I can't express how much I want these. It seems as if they supplied something to my brain that it cannot bear, when busy, to lose. For a week or a fortnight I can write prodigiously in a retired place (as at Broadstairs) and a day in London sets me up again and starts me. But the toil and labour of writing, day after day, without that magic lantern, is IMMENSE. I don't say this at all in low spirits, for we are perfectly comfortable here, and I like the place very much indeed, and the people are even more friendly and fond of me than they were in Genoa. I only mention it as a curious fact that I have never had an opportunity of finding out before. *My* figures seem to stagnate without crowds about them. I wrote very little in Genoa, (only *The Chimes*) and fancied myself conscious of some influence there – but Lord! I had two miles of streets at least, to walk about in, and a great theatre to repair to, every night.

After a short interval, he wrote again:

The absence of any accessible streets continues to worry me, now that I have so much to do, in a most singular manner. I should not walk in them in the daytime, if they were here, I dare say; but at night I want them beyond description. I don't seem to be able to get rid of my spectres unless I can lose them in crowds.

However, as you say, there are streets in Paris, and good suggestive streets too; and trips to London will be nothing then.

In this same letter he also described how he had been reading his first Dombey *chapters to an appreciative circle of friends in Lausanne, and jokingly suggested to Forster that he should engage Saint James's Hall! Then, later, in reply to Forster's half-earnest uneasiness, Dickens admitted that perhaps Covent Garden 'might be a little too large for my purpose'.*

Little did even the apprehensive Forster guess what huge theatres and halls would be filled to bursting for those readings, some of the most spectacular being in Paris.

Paris

It was in Paris, where Dickens moved with his family after their stay in Lausanne, that he wrote of the death of little Paul Dombey, which affected him so deeply that he had to go out and walk the snowy streets all night. This must have been a very different kind of walk from those in which he tried to bring his 'spectres' to life. He had just done that, only too effectively. But this did not prevent him from rushing to meet Forster in the morning, and from then on spending a fortnight with his friend. 'With a dreadful insatiability', records Forster, 'we passed through every variety of sight-seeing, prisons, palaces, theatres, hospitals, the Morgue and the Lazare, as well as the Louvre, Versailles, St Cloud, and all the spots made memorable by the first revolution.'

Through the good offices of their friends, the English Macready and the French Régnier, they were made free of the green rooms of all the best theatres. And, of course, they met many literary celebrities – Dumas, Chateaubriand, Lamartine and Victor Hugo, whose great kindness and personal charm they were always to remember. 'I never saw', wrote Forster, 'upon any features so keenly intellectual such a soft and sweet gentility.'

The family stayed in Paris from November 1846 until February 1847. Dickens was hard at work on Dombey, *but as usual his emotional vitality spilled over also in letters describing not only social and theatrical events but minute details of domestic life – at this period including battles with the intense cold to which they were so unused. But neither in* Dombey and Son *nor in any other novel, including* A Tale of Two Cities, *has he left any true impressions of the Paris he came to know and love so well. Paris, with all its spectacular contrasts. Paris, where side-by-side with frivolities and the mere ups-and-downs of ordinary living, the unforgettable Morgue spoke to his own deeply divided personality. 'Travelling Abroad' is not the only one of his essays in which this obsession takes such a disproportionate place.*

From 1847 to 1853 Dickens was firmly based in London. His visits to Paris were probably only in the form of such short delightful expeditions as he described in 'A Flight' which, in 1851, he wrote for his new periodical, Household Words. *Here, as the following extract shows, there is no shadow over his delight in finding himself, by the wizardry of the newly-established railway, having been whirled so swiftly from London to Paris, now 'rattling over the pavement in a hackney cabriolet'.*

Surely, not the pavement of Paris? Yes, I think it is, too. I don't know any other place where there are all these high houses, all these haggard-looking wine-shops, all these billiard-tables, all these stocking-makers with flat red or yellow legs of wood for signboard, all these fuel shops with stacks of billets painted outside, and real billets sawing in the gutter, all these dirty corners of streets, all these cabinet pictures over doorways representing discreet matrons nursing babies . . .

The crowds in the streets, the lights in the shops and balconies, the elegance, variety and beauty of their decorations, the number of the theatres, the brilliant cafés with their windows thrown up high and their vivacious groups at little tables on the pavement, the light and glitter of the houses turned as it were inside out, soon convince me that it is no dream; that I am in Paris, however I got here. I stroll down the sparkling Palais Royal, up the Rue de Rivoli to the Place Vendôme . . .

I walk up to the Barrière de l'Etoile, sufficiently dazed by my flight to have a pleasant doubt of the reality of everything about me; of the lively crowd, the overhanging trees, the performing dogs, the hobby-horses, the beautiful perspectives of shining lamps; the hundred and one enclosures, where the singing is, the gleaming orchestras of azure and gold, and where a star-eyed Houri comes round with a box for voluntary offerings. So, I pass to my hotel, enchanted; sup, enchanted; go to bed, enchanted; pushing back this morning (if it really were this morning) into the remoteness of time, blessing the South-Eastern Company for realising the Arabian Nights in these prose days . . .

In Provincial France

In the six years that Dickens was based in London and during which he was writing David Copperfield *and* Bleak House, *family holidays were spent in Brighton, the Isle of Wight and 'Our English Watering-Place', Broadstairs.*

In the summer of 1853, however, Dickens decided for a change to take the family to Boulogne which they liked so much that they spent the two following summers there also.

OUR FRENCH WATERING-PLACE

Having earned by many years of fidelity, the right to be sometimes inconstant to our English watering-place, we have dallied for two or three seasons with a French watering-place: once solely known to us as a town with a very long street, beginning with an abattoir and ending with a steam-boat, which it seemed our fate to behold only at daybreak on winter mornings, when (in the days before continental rail-roads), just sufficiently awake to know that we were most uncomfortably asleep, it was our destiny always to clatter through it, in the coupé of the diligence from Paris, with a sea of mud behind us, and a sea of tumbling waves before. In relation to which latter monster, our mind's eye now recalls a worthy Frenchman in a seal-skin cap with a braided hood over it, once our travelling companion in the coupé aforesaid, who, waking up with a pale and crumpled visage, and looking ruefully out at the grim row of breakers enjoying themselves fanatically on an instrument of torture called 'the Bar,' inquired of us whether we were ever sick at sea? Both to prepare his mind for the abject creature we were presently to become, and also to afford him consolation, we replied, 'Sir, your servant is always sick when it is possible to be so.' He returned, altogether uncheered by the bright example, 'Ah, Heaven, but I am always sick, even when it is *im*possible to be so.'

The means of communication between the French capital and our French watering-place are wholly changed since those days; but the Channel remains unbridged as yet, and the old floundering and knocking about go on there. It must be confessed that saving in reasonable (and therefore rare) sea-weather, the act of arrival at our French watering-place from England is difficult to be achieved with dignity. Several little circumstances combine to render the visitor an object of humiliation. In the first place, the steamer no sooner touches the port, than all the passengers fall into captivity: being boarded by an overpowering force of Custom-house officers, and marched into a gloomy dungeon. In the second place, the road to this dungeon is fenced off with ropes breast-high, and outside those ropes all the English in the place who have lately been sea-sick and are now well, assemble in their best clothes to enjoy the degradation of their dilapidated fellow-creatures. 'Oh, my gracious! how ill this one has been!' 'Here's a damp one coming next!' '*Here's* a pale one!' 'Oh! Ain't he green in the face, this next one!' Even we ourself (not deficient in natural dignity) have a lively remembrance of staggering up this detested lane one September day in a gale of wind, when we were received like an irresistible comic actor, with a burst of laughter and applause, occasioned by the extreme imbecility of our legs.

We were coming to the third place. In the third place, the captives, being shut up in the gloomy dungeon, are strained, two or three at a time, into an inner cell, to be examined as to passports; and across the doorway of communication, stands a military creature making a bar of his arm. Two ideas are generally present to the British mind during these ceremonies; first, that it is necessary to make for the cell with violent struggles, as if it were a life-boat and the dungeon a ship going down; secondly, that the military creature's arm is a national affront, which the government at home ought instantly to 'take up'. The British mind and body becoming heated by these fantasies, delirious answers are made to inquiries, and extravagant actions performed. Thus, Johnson persists in giving Johnson as his baptismal name, and substituting for his ancestral designation the national 'Dam!' Neither can he by any means be brought to recognise the distinction between a portmanteau-key and a passport, but will obstinately persevere in tendering the one when asked for the other. This brings him to the fourth place, in a state of mere idiocy; and when he is, in the fourth place, cast out at a little door into a howling wilderness of touters, he becomes a lunatic with wild eyes and floating hair until rescued and soothed. If friendless and unrescued, he is generally put into a railway omnibus and taken to Paris.

But our French watering-place, when it is once got into, is a very enjoyable place. It has a varied and beautiful country around it, and many characteristic and agreeable things within it. To be sure, it might have fewer bad smells and less decaying refuse, and it might be better drained, and much cleaner in many parts, and therefore infinitely more healthy. Still, it is a bright, airy, pleasant, cheerful town; and if you were to walk down either of its three well-paved main streets, towards five o'clock in the afternoon, when delicate odours of cookery fill the air, and its hotel windows (it is full of hotels) give glimpses of long tables set out for dinner, and made to look sumptuous by the aid of napkins folded fan-wise, you would rightly judge it to be an uncommonly good town to eat and drink in.

We have an old walled town, rich in cool public wells of water, on the top of a hill within and above the present business-town; and if it were some hundreds of miles further from England, instead of being, on a clear day, within sight of the grass growing in the crevices of the chalk-cliffs of Dover, you would long ago have been bored to death about that town. It is more picturesque and quaint than half the innocent places which tourists, following their leader like sheep, have made impostors of. To say nothing of its houses with grave courtyards, its queer by-corners, and its many-windowed streets white and quiet in the sunlight, there is an ancient belfry in it that would have been in all the Annuals and Albums, going and gone, these hundred years, if it had but been more expensive to get at. Happily it has escaped so well, being only in our French watering-place, that you may like it of your own accord in a natural manner, without being required to go into convulsions about it. We regard it as one of the later blessings of our life, that BILKINS, the only authority on Taste, never took any notice that we can find out, of our French watering-place. Bilkins never wrote about it, never pointed out anything to be seen in it, never measured anything in it, always left it alone. For which relief, Heaven bless the town and the memory of the immortal Bilkins likewise!

There is a charming walk, arched and shaded by trees, on the old walls that form the four sides of this High Town, whence you get glimpses of the streets below, and changing views of the other town and of the river, and of the hills and of the sea. It is made more agreeable and peculiar by some of the solemn houses that are rooted in the deep streets below, bursting into a fresher existence a-top, and having doors and windows, and even gardens, on these ramparts. A child going in at the courtyard gate of one of these houses, climbing up the many stairs, and coming out at the fourth-floor window, might conceive himself another Jack, alighting on enchanted ground from another bean-stalk. It is a place wonderfully populous in children; English children, with governesses reading novels as they walk down the shady lanes of trees, or nursemaids interchanging gossip on the seats; French children with their smiling bonnes in snow-white caps, and themselves – if little boys – in straw headgear like beehives, work-baskets and church hassocks. Three years ago, there were three weazen old men, one bearing a frayed red ribbon in his thread-bare button-hole, always to be found walking together among these children, before dinner-time. If they walked for an appetite, they doubtless lived en pension – were contracted for – otherwise their poverty would have made it a rash action. They were stooping, blear-eyed, dull old men, slip-shod and shabby, in long-skirted short-waisted coats and meagre trousers, and yet with a ghost of gentility hovering in their company. They spoke little to each other, and looked as if they might have been politically discontented if they had had vitality enough. Once, we overheard

La Morgue, Quai Notre Dame, Paris

red-ribbon feebly complain to the other two that somebody, or something, was 'a Robber;' and then they all three set their mouths so that they would have ground their teeth if they had had any. The ensuing winter gathered red-ribbon unto the great company of faded ribbons, and next year the remaining two were there – getting themselves entangled with hoops and dolls – familiar mysteries to the children – probably in the eyes of most of them, harmless creatures who had never been like children, and whom children could never be like. Another winter came, and another old man went, and so, this present year, the last of the triumvirate left off walking – it was no good, now – and sat by himself on a little solitary bench, with the hoops and the dolls as lively as ever all about him.

In the Place d'Armes of this town, a little decayed market is held, which seems to slip through the old gateway, like water, and go rippling down the hill, to mingle with the murmuring market in the lower town, and get lost in its movement and bustle. It is very agreeable on an idle summer morning to pursue this market-stream from the hill-top. It begins, dozingly and dully, with a few sacks of corn; starts into a surprising collection of boots and shoes; goes brawling down the hill in a diversified channel of old cordage, old iron, old crockery, old clothes, civil and military, old rags, new cotton goods, flaming prints of saints, little looking-glasses, and incalculable lengths of tape; dives into a backway, keeping out of sight for a little while, as streams will, or only sparkling for a moment in the shape of a market drinking-shop; and suddenly reappears behind the great church, shooting itself into a bright confusion of white-capped women and blue-bloused men, poultry, vegetables, fruits, flowers, pots, pans, praying-chairs, soldiers, country butter, umbrellas and other sun-shades, girl-porters waiting to be hired with baskets at their backs, and one weazen little old man in a cocked hat, wearing a cuirass of drinking-glasses and carrying on his shoulder a crimson temple fluttering with flags, like a glorified pavior's rammer without the handle, who rings a little bell in all parts of the scene, and cries his cooling drink Hola, Hola, Ho-o-o! in a shrill cracked voice that somehow makes itself heard, above all the chaffering and vending hum. Early in the afternoon, the whole course of the stream is dry. The praying-chairs are put back in the church, the umbrellas are folded up, the unsold goods are carried away, the stalls and stands disappear, the square is swept, the hackney coaches lounge there to be hired, and on all the country roads (if you walk about, as much as we do) you will see the peasant women, always neatly and comfortably dressed, riding home, with the pleasantest saddle-furniture of clean milk-pails, bright butter-kegs, and the like, on the jolliest little donkeys in the world.

We have another market in our French watering-place – that is to say, a few wooden hutches in the open street, down by the Port – devoted to fish. Our fishing-boats are famous everywhere; and our fishing people, though they love lively colours and taste is neutral (see Bilkins), are among the most picturesque people we ever encountered. They have not only a quarter of their own in the town itself, but they occupy whole villages of their own on the neighbouring cliffs. Their churches and chapels are their own; they consort with one another, they intermarry among themselves, their customs are their own, and their costume is their own and never changes. As soon as one of their boys can walk, he is provided with a long bright red nightcap; and one of their men would as soon think of going afloat without his head, as without that indispensable appendage to it. Then, they wear the noblest boots, with the hugest tops – flapping and bulging over anyhow; above which, they encase themselves in such wonderful overalls and petticoat trousers, made to all appearance of tarry old sails, so additionally stiffened with pitch and salt, that the wearers have a walk of their own, and go straddling and swinging about among the boats and barrels and nets and rigging, a sight to see. Then, their younger women, by dint of going down to the sea barefoot, to fling their baskets into the boats as they come in with the tide, and bespeak the first fruits of the haul with propitiatory promises to love and marry that dear fisherman who shall fill that basket like an Angel, have the finest legs ever carved by Nature in the brightest mahogany, and they walk like Juno. Their eyes, too, are so lustrous that their long gold ear-rings turn dull beside those brilliant neighbours;

and when they are dressed, what with these beauties, and their fine fresh faces, and their many petticoats – striped petticoats, red petticoats, blue petticoats, always clean and smart, and never too long – and their home-made stockings, mulberry-coloured, blue, brown, purple, lilac – which the older women, taking care of the Dutch-looking children, sit in all sorts of places knitting, knitting, knitting from morning to night – and what with their little saucy bright blue jackets, knitted too, and fitting close to their handsome figures; and what with the natural grace with which they wear the commonest cap, or fold the commonest handkerchief round their luxuriant hair – we say, in a word and out of breath, that taking all these premises into our consideration, it has never been a matter of the least surprise to us that we have never once met, in the cornfields, on the dusty roads, by the breezy windmills, on the plots of short sweet grass overhanging the sea – anywhere – a young fisherman and fisherwoman of our French watering-place together, but the arm of that fisherman has invariably been, as a matter of course and without any absurd attempt to disguise so plain a necessity, round the neck or waist of that fisherwoman. And we have had no doubt whatever, standing looking at their uphill streets, house rising about house, and terrace above terrace, and bright garments here and there lying sunning on rough stone parapets, that the pleasant mist on all such objects, caused by their being seen through the brown nets hung across on poles to dry, is, in the eyes of every true young fisherman, a mist of love and beauty, setting off the goddess of his heart.

Moreover it is to be observed that these are an industrious people, and a domestic people, and an honest people. And though we are aware that at the bidding of Bilkins it is our duty to fall down and worship the Neapolitans, we make bold very much to prefer the fishing people of our French watering-place – especially since our last visit to Naples within these twelve months, when we found only four conditions of men remaining in the whole city: to wit, lazzaroni, priests, spies, and soldiers, and all of them beggars; the paternal government having banished all its subjects except the rascals.

But we can never henceforth separate our French watering-place from our own landlord of two summers, M. Loyal Devasseur, citizen and town-councillor. Permit us to have the pleasure of presenting M. Loyal Devasseur.

His own family name is simply Loyal; but as he is married, and as in that part of France a husband always adds to his own name the family name of his wife, he writes himself Loyal Devasseur. He owns a compact little estate of some twenty or thirty acres on a lofty hill-side, and on it he has built two country houses, which he lets furnished. They are by many degrees the best houses that are so let near our French watering-place; we have had the honour of living in both, and can testify. The entrance-hall of the first we inhabited was ornamented with a plan of the estate, representing it as about twice the size of Ireland; insomuch that when we were yet new to the property (M. Loyal always speaks of it as 'La propriété') we went three miles straight on end in search of the bridge of Austerlitz – which we afterwards found to be immediately outside the window. The Château of the Old Guard, in another part of the grounds, and according to the plan, about two leagues from the little dining-room, we sought in vain for a week, until, happening one evening to sit upon a bench in the forest (forest in the plan), a few yards from the house-door, we observed at our feet, in the ignominious circumstances of being upside down and greenly rotten, the Old Guard himself: that is to say, the painted effigy of a member of that distinguished corps, seven feet high, and in the act of carrying arms, who had had the misfortune to be blown down in the previous winter. It will be perceived that M. Loyal is a staunch admirer of the great Napoleon. He is an old soldier himself – captain of the National Guard, with a handsome gold vase on his chimney-piece, presented to him by his company – and his respect for the memory of the illustrious general is enthusiastic. Medallions of him, portraits of him, busts of him, pictures of him, are thickly sprinkled all over the property. During the first month of our occupation, it was our affliction to be constantly knocking down Napoleon: if we touched a shelf in a dark corner, he toppled over with a crash; and every door we opened, shook him to the soul. Yet M. Loyal is not a man of mere castles in the air, or, as he would say, in Spain. He has a specially practical, contriving, clever, skilful eye and hand. His houses are delightful. He unites French elegance and English comfort, in a happy manner quite his own. He has an extraordinary genius for making tasteful little bedrooms in angles of his roofs, which an Englishman would as soon think of turning to any account as he would think of cultivating the Desert. We have ourself reposed deliciously in an elegant chamber of M. Loyal's construction, with our head as nearly in the kitchen chimney-pot as we can conceive it likely for the head of any gentleman, not by profession a Sweep, to be. And into whatsoever strange nook M. Loyal's genius penetrates, it, in that nook, infallibly constructs a cupboard and a row of pegs. In either of our houses, we could have put away the knapsacks, and hung up the hats of the whole regiment of Guides.

Aforetime, M. Loyal was a tradesman in the town. You can transact business with no present tradesman in the town, and give your card 'chez M. Loyal,' but a brighter face shines upon you directly. We doubt if there is, ever was, or ever will be, a man so universally pleasant in the minds of people as M. Loyal is in the minds of the citizens of our French watering-place. They rub their hands and laugh when they speak of him. Ah, but he is such a good child, such a brave boy, such a generous spirit, that Monsieur Loyal! It is the honest truth. M. Loyal's nature is the nature of a gentleman. He cultivates his ground with his own hands (assisted by one little labourer, who falls into a fit now and then); and he digs and delves from morn to eve in prodigious perspirations – 'works always,' as he says – but, cover him with dust, mud, weeds, water, any stains you will, you never can cover the gentleman in M. Loyal. A portly, upright, broad-shouldered, brown faced man, whose soldierly bearing gives him the appearance of being taller than he is, look into the bright eye of M. Loyal, standing before you in his working-blouse and cap, not particularly well shaved, and, it may be, very earthy, and you shall discern in M. Loyal a gentleman whose true politeness is in grain, and confirmation of whose word by his bond you would blush to think of. Not without reason is M. Loyal when he tells that story, in his own vivacious way, of his travelling to Fulham, near London, to buy all these hundreds and hundreds of trees you now see upon the Property, than a bare, bleak hill; and of his sojourning in Fulham three months; and of his jovial evenings with the market-gardeners; and of the crowning banquet before his departure, when the market-gardeners rose as one man, clinked their glasses all together (as the custom at Fulham is), and cried, 'Vive Loyal!'

M. Loyal has an agreeable wife, but no family; and he loves to drill the children of his tenants, or run races with them, or do anything with them, or for them, that is good-natured. He is of a highly convivial temperament, and his hospitality is unbounded. Billet a soldier on him, and he is delighted. Five-and-thirty soldiers had M. Loyal billeted on him this present summer, and they all got fat and red-faced in two days. It became a legend among the troops that whosoever got billeted on M. Loyal rolled in clover; and so it fell out that the fortunate man who drew the billet 'M. Loyal Devasseur' always leaped into the air, though in heavy marching order. M. Loyal cannot bear to admit anything that might seem by any implication to disparage the military profession. We hinted to him once, that we were conscious of a remote doubt arising in our mind, whether a sou a day for pocket-money, tobacco, stockings, drink, washing, and social pleasures in general, left a very large margin for a soldier's enjoyment. Pardon! said Monsieur Loyal, rather wincing. It was not a fortune, but – à la bonne heure – it was better than it used to be! What, we asked him on another occasion, were all those neighbouring peasants, each living with his family in one room, and each having a soldier (perhaps two) billeted on him every other night, required to provide for those soldiers? 'Faith!' said M. Loyal, reluctantly; 'a bed, monsieur, and fire to cook with, and a candle. And they share their supper with those soldiers. It is not possible that they could eat alone.' – 'And what allowance do they get for this?' said we, Monsieur Loyal drew himself up taller, took a step back, laid his hand upon his breast, and said, with majesty, as speaking for himself and all France, 'Monsieur, it is a contribution to the State!'

It is never going to rain, according to M. Loyal. When it is impossible to deny that it is now raining in torrents, he says it will be fine – charming – magnificent – to-morrow. It is never hot on the Property, he contends. Likewise it is never cold. The flowers, he says, come out, delighting to grow there; it is like Paradise this morning; it is like the Garden of Eden. He is a little fanciful in his language: smilingly observing of Madame Loyal, when she is absent at vespers, that she is 'gone to her salvation' – allée à son salut. He has a great enjoyment of tobacco, but nothing would induce him to continue smoking face to face with a lady. His short black pipe immediately goes into his breast pocket, scorches his blouse, and nearly sets him on fire. In the Town Council and on occasions of ceremony, he appears in a full suit of black, with a waistcoat of magnificent breadth across the chest, and a shirt-collar of fabulous proportions. Good M. Loyal! Under blouse or waistcoat, he carries one of the gentlest hearts that beat in a nation teeming with gentle people. He has had losses, and has been at his best under them. Not only the loss of his way by night in the Fulham times – when a bad subject of an Englishman, under pretence of seeing him home, took him into all the night public-houses, drank 'arfanarf' in every one at his expense, and finally fled, leaving him shipwrecked at Cleefee-way, which we apprehend to be Ratcliffe Highway – but heavier losses than that. Long ago a family of children and a mother were left in one of his houses without money, a whole year. M. Loyal – anything but as rich as we wish he had been – had not the heart to say 'you must go;' so they stayed on and stayed on, and paying-tenants who would have come in couldn't come in, and at last they managed to get helped home across the water; and M. Loyal kissed the whole group, and said, 'Adieu, my poor infants!' and sat down in their deserted salon and smoked his pipe of peace. – 'The rent, M. Loyal?' 'Eh! well! The rent!' M. Loyal shakes his head. 'Le bon Dieu,' says M. Loyal presently, will recompense me,' and he laughs and smokes his pipe of peace. May he smoke it on the Property, and not be recompensed, these fifty years!

There are public amusements in our French watering-place,

or it would not be French. They are very popular, and very cheap. The sea-bathing – which may rank as the most favoured daylight entertainment, inasmuch as the French visitors bathe all day long, and seldom appear to think of remaining less than an hour at a time in the water – is astoundingly cheap. Omnibuses convey you, if you please, from a convenient part of the town to the beach and back again; you have a clean and comfortable bathing-machine, dress, linen, and all appliances; and the charge for the whole is half-a-franc, or fivepence. On the pier, there is usually a guitar, which seems presumptuously enough to set its tinkling against the deep hoarseness of the sea, and there is always some boy or woman who sings, without any voice, little songs without any tune: the strain we have most frequently heard being an appeal to 'the sportsman' not to bag that choicest of game, the swallow. For bathing purposes, we have also a subscription establishment with an esplanade, where people lounge about with telescopes, and seem to get a good deal of weariness for their money; and we have also an association of individual machine proprietors combined against this formidable rival. M. Féroce, our own particular friend in the bathing line, is one of these. How he ever came by his name we cannot imagine. He is as gentle and polite a man as M. Loyal Devasseur himself; immensely stout withal, and of a beaming aspect. M. Féroce has saved so many people from drowning, and has been decorated with so many medals in consequence, that his stoutness seems a special dispensation of Providence to enable him to wear them; if his girth were the girth of an ordinary man, he could never hang them on, all at once. It is only on very great occasions that M. Féroce displays his shining honours. At other times they lie by, with rolls of manuscript testifying to the causes of their presentation, in a huge glass case in the red-sofa'd salon of his private residence on the beach, where M. Féroce also keeps his family pictures, his portraits of himself as he appears both in bathing life and in private life, his little boats that rock by clock-work, and his other ornamental possessions.

Then, we have a commodious and gay Theatre – or had, for it is burned down now – where the opera was always preceded by a vaudeville, in which (as usual) everybody, down to the little old man with the large hat and the little cane and tassel, who always played either my Uncle or my Papa, suddenly broke out of the dialogue into the mildest vocal snatches to the great perplexity of unaccustomed strangers from Great Britain, who never could make out when they were singing and when they were talking – and indeed it was pretty much the same. But the caterers in the way of entertainment to whom we are most beholden are the Society of Welldoing, who are active all the summer, and give the proceeds of their good works to the poor. Some of the most agreeable fêtes they contrive are announced as 'Dedicated to the children;' and the taste with which they turn a small public enclosure into an elegant garden beautifully illuminated, and the thorough-going heartiness and energy with which they personally direct the childish pleasures, are supremely delightful. For fivepence a head, we have on these occasions donkey races with English 'Jokeis,' and other rustic sports; lotteries for toys, roundabouts, dancing on the grass to the music of an admirable band, fire-balloons and fireworks. Further, almost every week all through the summer – never mind, now, on what day of the week – there is a fête in some adjoining village (called in that part of the country a Ducasse), where the people – really *the people* – dance on the green turf in the open air, round a little orchestra, that seems itself to dance, there is such an airy motion of flags and streamers all about it. And we do not suppose that between the Torrid Zone and the North Pole there are to be found male dancers with such astonishingly loose legs, furnished with so many joints in wrong places, utterly unknown to Professor Owen, as those who here disport themselves. Sometimes the fête appertains to a particular trade; you will see among the cheerful young women at the joint Ducasse of the milliners and tailors, a wholesome knowledge of the art of making common and cheap things uncommon and pretty, by good sense and good taste, that is a practical lesson to any rank of society in a whole island we could mention. The oddest feature of these agreeable scenes is the everlasting Roundabout (we preserve an English word wherever we can, as we are writing the English language), on the wooden horses of which machine grown-up people of all ages are wound round and round with the utmost solemnity, while the proprietor's wife grinds an organ, capable of only one tune, in the centre.

As to the boarding-houses of our French watering-place, they are Legion, and would require a distinct treatise. It is not without a sentiment of national pride that we believe them to contain more bores from the shores of Albion than all the clubs in London. As you walk timidly in their neighbourhood, the very neckcloths and hats of your elderly compatriots cry to you from the stones of the streets, 'We are Bores – avoid us!' We have never overheard at street corners such lunatic scraps of political and social discussion as among these dear countrymen of ours. They believe everything that is impossible and nothing that is true. They carry rumours, and ask questions, and make corrections and improvements on one another, staggering to the human intellect. And they are for ever rushing into the English library, propounding such incomprehensible paradoxes to the fair mistress of that establishment, that we beg to recommend her to her Majesty's gracious consideration as a fit object for a pension.

The English form a considerable part of the population of our French watering-place, and are deservedly addressed and respected in many ways. Some of the surface-addresses to them are odd enough, as when a laundress puts a placard outside her house announcing her possession of that curious British instrument, a 'Mingle;' or when a tavern-keeper provides accommodation for the celebrated English game of 'Nokemdon.' But, to us, it is not the least pleasant feature of our French watering-place that a long and constant fusion of the two great nations there has taught each to like the other, and to learn from the other, and to rise superior to the absurd prejudices that have lingered among the weak and ignorant in both countries equally.

Drumming and trumpeting of course go on for ever in our French watering-place. Flag-flying is at a premium, too; but we cheerfully avow that we consider a flag a very pretty object, and that we take such outward signs of innocent liveliness to our heart of hearts. The people, in the town and in the country, are a busy people who work hard; they are sober, temperate, good-humoured, light-hearted, and generally remarkable for their engaging manners. Few just men, not immoderately bilious, could see them in their recreations without very much respecting the character that is so easily, so harmlessly, and so simply, pleased.

In a letter to Forster of 26 June, Dickens drew a delightful true-to-life picture of his landlord.

MONSIEUR BEAUCOURT

But the landlord – M. Beaucourt – is wonderful. Everybody here has two surnames (I cannot conceive why), and M. Beaucourt, as he is always called, is by rights M. Beaucourt-Mutuel. He is a portly jolly fellow with a fine open face; lives on the hill behind, just outside the top of the garden; and was a linen draper in the town, where he still has a shop, but is supposed to have mortgaged his business and to be in difficulties – all along of this place, which he has planted with his own hands; which he cultivates all day; and which he never on any consideration speaks of but as 'the property.' He is extraordinarily popular in Boulogne (the people in the shops invariably brightening up at the mention of his name, and congratulating us on being his tenants), and really seems to deserve it. He is such a liberal fellow that I can't bear to ask him for anything, since he instantly supplies it whatever it is. The things he has done in respect of unreasonable bedsteads and washing-stands, I blush to think of. I observed the other day in one of the side gardens – there are gardens at each side of the house too – a place where I thought the 'Comic Countryman' (a name he was giving just then to his youngest boy) 'must infallibly trip over, and make a little descent of a dozen feet. So I said "M. Beaucourt" – who instantly pulled off his cap and stood bareheaded – "there are some spare pieces of wood lying by the cow-house, if you would have the kindness to have one laid across here I think it would be safer." "Ah, mon Dieu sir," said M. Beaucourt, "it must be iron. This is not a portion of the property where you would like to see wood." "But iron is so expensive," said I, "and it really is not worth while——" "Sir, pardon me a thousand times," said M. Beaucourt, "it shall be iron. Assuredly and perfectly it shall be iron." "Then M. Beaucourt," said I, "I shall be glad to pay a moiety of the cost." "Sir," said M. Beaucourt, "Never!" Then to change the subject, he slided from his firmness and gravity into a graceful conversational tone, and said, "In the moonlight last night, the flowers on the property appeared, O heaven, to be *bathing themselves in the sky*. You like the property?" "M. Beaucourt," said I, "I am enchanted with it; I am more than satisfied with everything." "And I sir," said M. Beaucourt, laying his cap upon his breast, and kissing his hand – "I equally!" Yesterday two blacksmiths came for a day's work, and put up a good solid handsome bit of iron-railing, mortised into the stone parapet. . . . If the extraordinary things in the house defy description, the amazing phenomena in the gardens never could have been dreamed of by anybody but a Frenchman bent upon one idea. Besides a portrait of the house in the dining-room, there is a plan of the property in the hall. It looks about the size of Ireland; and to every one of the extraordinary objects there is a reference with some portentous name. There are fifty-one such references, including the Cottage of Tom Thumb, the Bridge of Austerlitz, the Bridge of Jena, the Hermitage, the Bower of the Old Guard, the Labyrinth (I have no idea which is which); and there is guidance to every room in the house, as if it were a place on that stupendous scale that without such a clue you must infallibly lose your way, and perhaps perish of starvation between bedroom and bedroom.'

On 3 July there came a fresh trait of the good fellow of a landlord. 'Fancy what Beaucourt told me last night. When he "conceived the inspiration" of planting the property ten years ago, he went over to England to buy the trees, took a small cottage in the market-gardens at Putney, lived there three months, held a symposium every night attended by the principal gardners of Fulham, Putney, Kew, and Hammersmith (which he calls Hamsterdam), and wound up with a supper at which the market-gardeners rose, clinked their glasses, and exclaimed with one accord (I quote him exactly) VIVE BEAUCOURT! He was a captain in the National Guard, and Cavaignac his general. Brave Capitaine Beaucourt! said Cavaignac, you must receive a decoration. My General, said Beaucourt, No! It is enough for me that I have done my duty. I go to lay the first stone of a house upon a Property I have – that house shall be my decoration. (Regard that house!)' Addition to the picture came in a letter of 24 July; with a droll glimpse of Shakespeare at the theatre, and of the Saturday's pig-market.

'I may mention that the great Beaucourt daily changes the orthography of this place. He has now fixed it, by having painted up outside the garden gate, "Entrée particulière de la Villa des Moulineaux." On another gate a little higher up, he has had painted "Entré des Ecuries de la Villa des Moulineaux." On another gate a little lower down (applicable to one of the innumerable buildings in the garden), "Entrée du Tom Pouce." On the highest gate of the lot, leading to his own house, "Entrée du Château Napoléonienne." All of which inscriptions you will behold in black and white when you come. I see little of him now, as, all things being "bien arrangées," he is delicate of appearing. His wife has been making a trip in the country during the last three weeks, but (as he mentioned to me with his hat in his hand) it was necessary that he should remain here, to be continually at the disposition of the tenant of the Property. (The better to do this, he has had roaring dinner parties of fifteen daily; and the old woman who milks the cows has been fainting up the hill under vast burdens of champagne.)

Later on, a typically 'Uncommercial' fantasy appeared in his periodical, All the Year Round.

IN THE FRENCH-FLEMISH COUNTRY

'It is neither a bold nor a diversified country,' said I to myself, 'this country which is three-quarters Flemish, and a quarter French; yet it has its attractions too. Though great lines of railway traverse it, the trains leave it behind, and go puffing off to Paris and the South, to Belgium and Germany, to the Northern Sea-Coast of France, and to England, and merely smoke it a little in passing. Then I don't know it, and that is a good reason for being here; and I can't pronounce half the long queer names I see inscribed over the shops, and that is another good reason for being here, since I surely ought to learn how.' In short, I was 'here,' and I wanted an excuse for not going away from here, and I made it to my satisfaction, and stayed here.

What part in my decision was borne by Monsieur P. Salcy, is of no moment, though I own to encountering that gentleman's name on a red bill on the wall, before I made up my mind. Monsieur P. Salcy, 'par permission de M. le Maire,' had established his theatre in the whitewashed Hôtel de Ville, on the steps of which illustrious edifice I stood. And Monsieur P. Salcy, privileged director of such theatre, situate in 'the first theatrical arrondissement of the department of the North,' invited French-Flemish mankind to come and partake of the intellectual banquet provided by his family of dramatic artists, fifteen subjects in number. 'La Famille P. SALCY, composée d'artistes dramatiques, au nombre de 15 sujets.'

Neither a bold nor a diversified country, I say again, and withal an untidy country, but pleasant enough to ride in, when the paved roads over the flats and through the hollows, are not too deep in black mud. A country so sparely inhabited, that I wonder where the peasants who till and sow and reap the ground, can possibly dwell, and also by what invisible balloons they are conveyed from their distant homes into the fields at sunrise and back again at sunset. The occasional few poor cottages and farms in this region, surely cannot afford shelter to the numbers necessary to the cultivation, albeit the work is done so very deliberately, that on one long harvest day I have seen, in twelve miles, about twice as many men and women (all told) reaping and binding. Yet have I seen more cattle, more sheep, more pigs, and all in better case, than where there is purer French spoken, and also better ricks – round swelling peg-top ricks, well thatched: not a shapeless brown heap, like the toast of a Giant's toast-and-water, pinned to the earth with one of the skewers out of his kitchen. A good custom they have about here, likewise, of prolonging the sloping tiled roof of farm or cottage, so that it overhangs three or four feet, carrying off the wet, and making a good drying-place wherein to hang up herbs, or implements, or what not. A better custom than the popular one of keeping the refuse-heap and puddle close before the house door: which, although I paint my dwelling never so brightly blue (and it cannot be too blue for me, hereabouts), will bring fever inside my door. Wonderful poultry of the French-Flemish country, why take the trouble to *be* poultry? Why not stop short at eggs in the rising generation, and die out and have done with it? Parents of chickens have I seen this day, followed by their wretched young families, scratching nothing out of the mud with an air – tottering about on legs so scraggy and weak, that the valiant word drumsticks becomes a mockery when applied to them, and the crow of the lord and master has been a mere dejected case of croup. Carts have I seen, and other agricultural instruments, unwieldy, dislocated, monstrous. Poplar-trees by the thousand fringe the fields and fringe the end of the flat landscape, so that I feel, looking straight on before me, as if, when I pass the extremest fringe on the low horizon, I shall tumble over into space. Little whitewashed black holes of chapels, with barred doors and Flemish inscriptions, abound at roadside corners, and often they are garnished with a sheaf of wooden crosses, like children's swords; or, in their default, some hollow old tree with a saint roosting in it, similarly decorated, or a pole with a very diminutive saint enshrined aloft in a sort of sacred pigeon-house. Not that we are deficient in such decoration in the town here, for, over at the church yonder, outside the building, is a scenic representation of the Crucifixion, built up with old bricks and stones, and made out with painted canvas and wooden figures: the whole surmounting the dusty skull of some holy personage (perhaps), shut up behind a little ashy iron grate, as if it were originally put there to be cooked, and the fire had long gone out. A windmilly country this, though the windmills are so damp and rickety, that they nearly knock themselves off their legs at every turn of their sails, and creak in loud complaint. A weaving country, too, for in the wayside cottages the loom goes wearily – rattle and click, rattle and click – and, looking in, I see the poor weaving peasant, man or woman, bending at the work, while the child, working too, turns a little handwheel put upon the ground to suit its height. An unconscionable monster, the loom in a small dwelling, asserting himself ungenerously as the bread-winner, straddling over the children's straw beds, cramping the family in space and air, and making himself generally objectionable and tyrannical. He is tributary, too, to ugly mills and factories and bleaching-grounds, rising out of the sluiced fields in an abrupt bare way, disdaining, like himself, to be ornamental or accommodating. Surrounded by these things, here I stood on the steps of the Hôtel de Ville, persuaded to remain by the P. Salcy family, fifteen dramatic subjects strong.

There was a Fair besides. The double persuasion being irresistible, and my sponge being left behind at the last Hotel, I made the tour of the little town to buy another. In the small sunny shops – mercers, opticians, and druggist-grocers, with here and there an emporium of religious images – the gravest of old spectacled Flemish husbands and wives sat contemplating one another across bare counters, while the wasps, who seemed to have taken military possession of the town, and to have placed it under wasp-martial law, executed warlike manœuvres in the windows. Other shops the wasps had entirely to themselves, and nobody cared and nobody came when I beat with a five-franc piece upon the board of custom. What I sought was no more to be found than if I had sought a nugget of Californian gold: so I went, spongeless, to pass the evening with the Family P. Salcy.

The members of the Family P. Salcy were so fat and so like one another – fathers, mothers, sisters, brothers, uncles, and aunts – that I think the local audience were much confused about the plot of the piece under representation, and to the last expected that everybody must turn out to be the long-lost relative of everybody else. The Theatre was established on the top story of the Hôtel de Ville, and was approached by a long bare staircase, whereon, in an airy situation, one of the P. Salcy Family –

a stout gentleman imperfectly repressed by a belt – took the money. This occasioned the greatest excitement of the evening; for, no sooner did the curtain rise on the introductory Vaudeville, and reveal in the person of the young lover (singing a very short song with his eyebrows) apparently the very same identical stout gentleman imperfectly repressed by a belt, than everybody rushed out to the paying-place, to ascertain whether he could possibly have put on that dress-coat, that clear complexion, and those arched black vocal eyebrows, in so short a space of time. It then became manifest that this was another stout gentleman imperfectly repressed by a belt: to whom, before the spectators had recovered their presence of mind, entered a third stout gentleman imperfectly repressed by a belt, exactly like him. These two 'subjects,' making with the money-taker three of the announced fifteen, fell into conversation touching a charming young widow: who, presently appearing, proved to be a stout lady altogether irrepressible by any means – quite a parallel case to the American Negro – fourth of the fifteen subjects, and sister of the fifth who presided over the check-department. In good time the whole of the fifteen subjects were dramatically presented, and we had the inevitable Ma Mère, Ma Mère! and also the inevitable malédiction d'un père, and likewise the inevitable Marquis, and also the inevitable provincial young man, weak-minded but faithful, who followed Julie to Paris, and cried and laughed and choked all at once. The story was wrought out with the help of a virtuous spinning-wheel in the beginning, a vicious set of diamonds in the middle, and a rheumatic blessing (which arrived by post) from Ma Mère towards the end; the whole resulting in a small sword in the body of one of the stout gentlemen imperfectly repressed by a belt, fifty thousand francs per annum and a decoration to the other stout gentleman imperfectly repressed by a belt, and an assurance from everybody to the provincial young man that if he were not supremely happy – which he seemed to have no reason whatever for being – he ought to be. This afforded him a final opportunity of crying and laughing and choking all at once, and sent the audience home sentimentally delighted. Audience more attentive or better behaved there could not possibly be, though the places of second rank in the Theatre of the Family P. Salcy were sixpence each in English money, and the places of first rank a shilling. How the fifteen subjects ever got so fat upon it, the kind Heavens know.

What gorgeous china figures of knights and ladies, gilded till they gleamed again, I might have bought at the Fair for the garniture of my home, if I had been a French-Flemish peasant, and had had the money! What a shining coffee-cups and saucers I might have won at the turntables, if I had had the luck! Ravishing perfumery also, and sweetmeats, I might have speculated in, or I might have fired for prizes at a multitude of little dolls in niches, and might have hit the doll of dolls, and won francs and fame. Or, being a French-Flemish youth, I might have been drawn in a handcart by my compeers, to tilt for municipal rewards at the water-quintain; which, unless I sent my lance clean through the ring, emptied a full bucket over me; to fend off which, the competitors wore grotesque old scarecrow hats. Or, being French-Flemish man or woman, boy or girl, I might have circled all night on my hobby-horse in a stately cavalcade of hobby-horses four abreast, interspersed with triumphal cars, going round and round and round and round, we the goodly company singing a ceaseless chorus to the music of the barrel-organ, drum, and cymbals. On the whole, not more monotonous than the Ring in Hyde Park, London, and much merrier; for when do the circling company sing chorus, *there*, to the barrel-organ, when do the ladies embrace their horses round the neck with both arms, when do the gentlemen fan the ladies with the tails of their gallant steeds? On all these revolving delights, and on their own especial lamps and Chinese lanterns revolving with them, the thoughtful weaver-face brightens, and the Hôtel de Ville sheds an illuminated line of gaslight: while above it, the Eagle of France, gas-outlined and apparently afflicted with the prevailing infirmities that have lighted on the poultry, is in a very undecided state of policy, and as a bird moulting. Flags flutter all around. Such is the prevailing gaiety that the keeper of the prison sits on the stone steps outside the prison-door, to have a look at the world that is not locked up; while that agreeable retreat, the wine-shop opposite to the prison in the prison-alley (its sign La Tranquillité, because of its charming situation), resounds with the voices of the shepherds and shepherdesses who resort there this festive night. And it reminds me that only this afternoon, I saw a shepherd in trouble, tending this way, over the jagged stones of a neighbouring street. A magnificent sight it was, to behold him in his blouse, a feeble little jog-trot rustic, swept along by the wind of two immense gendarmes, in cocked-hats for which the street was hardly wide enough, each carrying a bundle of stolen property that would not have held his shoulder-knot, and clanking a sabre that dwarfed the prisoner.

'Messieurs et Mesdames, I present to you at this Fair, as a mark of my confidence in the people of this so-renowned town, and as an act of homage to their good sense and fine taste, the Ventriloquist, the Ventriloquist! Further, Messieurs et Mesdames, I present to you the Face-Maker, the Physiognomist, the great Changer of Countenances, who transforms the features that Heaven has bestowed upon him into an endless succession of surprising and extraordinary visages, comprehending, Messieurs et Mesdames, all the contortions, energetic and expressive, of which the human face is capable, and all the passions of the human heart, as Love, Jealousy, Revenge, Hatred, Avarice, Despair! Hi hi, Ho ho, Lu lu, Come in!' To this effect, with an occasional smite upon a sonorous kind of tambourine – bestowed with a will, as if it represented the people who won't come in – holds forth a man of lofty and severe demeanour; a man in stately uniform, gloomy with the knowledge he possesses of the inner secrets of the booth. 'Come in, come in! Your opportunity presents itself to-night; to-morrow it will be gone for ever. To-morrow morning by the Express Train the railroad will reclaim the Ventriloquist and the Face-Maker! Algeria will reclaim the Ventriloquist and the Face-Maker! Yes! For the honour of their country they have accepted propositions of a magnitude incredible, to appear in Algeria. See them for the last time before their departure! We go to commence on the instant. Hi hi! Ho ho! Lu lu! Come in! Take the money that now ascends, Madame; but after that, no more, for we commence! Come in!'

Nevertheless, the eyes both of the gloomy Speaker and of Madame receiving sous in a muslin bower, survey the crowd pretty sharply after the ascending money has ascended, to detect any lingering sous at the turning-point. 'Come in, come in! Is there any more money, Madame, on the point of ascending? If so, we wait for it. If not, we commence!' The orator looks back over his shoulder to say it, lashing the spectators with the conviction that he beholds through the folds of the drapery into which he is about to plunge, the Ventriloquist and the Face-Maker. Several sous burst out of pockets, and ascend. 'Come up, then, Messieurs!' exlaims Madame in a shrill voice, and beckoning with a bejewelled finger. 'Come up! This presses. Monsieur has commanded that they commence!' Monsieur dives into his Interior, and the last half-dozen of us follow. His interior is comparatively severe; his Exterior also. A true Temple of Art needs nothing but seats, drapery, a small table with two moderator lamps hanging over it, and an ornamental looking-glass let into the wall. Monsieur in uniform gets behind the table and surveys us with disdain, his forehead becoming diabolically intellectual under the moderators. 'Messieurs et Mesdames, I present to you the Ventriloquist. He will commence with the celebrated Experience of the bee in the window. The bee, apparently the veritable bee of Nature, will hover in the window, and about the room. He will be with difficulty caught in the hand of Monsieur the Ventriloquist – he will escape – he will again hover – at length he will be recaptured by Monsieur the Ventriloquist, and will be with difficulty put into a bottle. Achieve then, Monsieur!' Here the proprietor is replaced behind the table by the Ventriloquist, who is thin and sallow, and of a weakly aspect. While the bee is in progress, Monsieur the Proprietor sits apart on a stool, immersed in dark and remote thought. The moment the bee is bottled, he stalks forward, eyes us gloomily as we applaud, and then announces, sternly waving his hand: 'The magnificent Experience of the child with the whooping-cough!' The child disposed of, he starts up as before. 'The superb and extraordinary Experience of the dialogue between Monsieur Tatambour in his dining-room, and his domestic, Jerome, in the cellar; concluding with the songsters of the grove, and the Concert of domestic Farm-yard animals.' All this done, and well done, Monsieur the Ventriloquist withdraws, and Monsieur the Face-Maker bursts in, as if his retiring-room were a mile long instead of a yard. A corpulent little man in a large white waistcoat, with a comic countenance, and with a wig in his hand. Irreverent disposition to laugh, instantly checked by the tremendous gravity of the Face-Maker, who intimates in his bow that if we expect that sort of thing we are mistaken. A very little shaving-glass with a leg behind it is handed in, and placed on the table before the Face-Maker. 'Messieurs et Mesdames, with no other assistance than this mirror and this wig, I shall have the honour of showing you a thousand characters.' As a preparation, the Face-Maker with both hands gouges himself, and turns his mouth inside out. He then becomes frightfully grave again, and says to the Proprietor, 'I am ready!' Proprietor stalks forth from baleful reverie, and announces 'The Young Conscript!' Face-Maker claps his wig on, hind side before, looks in the glass, and appears above it as a conscript so very imbecile, and squinting so extremely hard, that I should think the State would never get any good of him. Thunders of applause. Face-Maker dips behind the looking-glass, brings his own hair forward, is himself again, is awfully grave. 'A distinguished inhabitant of the Faubourg St. Germain.' Face-Maker dips, rises, is supposed to be aged, blear-eyed toothless, slightly palsied, supernaturally polite, evidently of noble birth. 'The oldest member of the Corps of Invalides on the fête-day of his master.' Face-Maker dips, rises, wears the wig on one side, has become the feeblest military bore in existence, and (it is clear) would lie frightfully about his past achievements, if he were not confined to pantomime. 'The Miser!' Face-Maker dips, rises, clutches a bag, and every hair of the wig is on end to express that he lives in continual dread of thieves. 'The Genius of France!' Face-Maker dips, rises, wig pushed back and smoothed flat, little cocked hat (artfully concealed till now) put a-top of it, Face-Maker's white waistcoat much advanced, Face-Maker's left hand in bosom of white waistcoat, Face-Maker's right hand behind his back. Thunders. This is the first of three positions of the Genius of France. In the second position, the Face-Maker takes snuff; in the third, rolls up his right hand, and surveys illimitable armies through that pocket-glass. The Face-Maker then, by putting out his tongue, and wearing the wig nohow in particular, becomes the Village Idiot. The most remarkable feature in the whole of his ingenious performance, is, that whatever he does to disguise himself, has the effect of rendering him rather more like himself than he was at first.

There were peep-shows in this Fair, and I had the pleasure of recognising several fields of glory with which I became well acquainted a year or two ago as Crimean battles, now doing duty as Mexican victories. The change was neatly effected by some extra smoking of the Russians, and by permitting the camp followers free range in the foreground to despoil the enemy of their uniforms. As no British troops had ever happened to be within sight when the artist took his original sketches, it followed fortunately that none were in the way now.

The Fair wound up with a ball. Respecting the particular night of the week on which the ball took place, I decline to commit myself; merely mentioning that it was held in a stable-yard so very close to the railway, that it is a mercy the locomotive did not set fire to it. (In Scotland, I suppose it would have done so.) There, in a tent prettily decorated with looking-glasses and a myriad of toy-flags, the people danced all night. It was not an expensive recreation, the price of a double ticket for a cavalier and lady being one and threepence in English money, and even of that small sum fivepence was reclaimable for 'consommation:' which word I venture to translate into refreshments of no greater strength, at the strongest, than ordinary wine made hot, with sugar and lemon in it. It was a ball of great good humour and of great enjoyment, though very many of the dancers must have been as poor as the fifteen subjects of the P. Salcy Family.

In short, not having taken my own pet national pint pot with me to this Fair, I was very well satisfied with the measure of simple enjoyment that it poured into the dull French-Flemish country life. How dull that is, I had an opportunity of considering when the Fair was over – when the tri-coloured flags were withdrawn from the windows of the houses on the Place where the Fair was held – when the windows were close shut, apparently until next Fair-time – when the Hôtel de Ville had cut off its gas and put away its eagle – when the two paviours, whom I take to form the entire paving population of the town, were ramming down the stones which had been pulled up for the erection of decorative poles – when the jailer had slammed his gate, and sulkily locked himself in with his charges. But then, as I paced the ring which marked the track of the departed hobby-horses on the market-place, pondering in my mind how long some hobby-horses do leave their tracks in public ways, and how difficult they are to erase, my eyes were greeted with a goodly sight. I beheld four male personages thoughtfully pacing the Place together, in the sunlight, evidently not belonging to the town, and having upon them a certain loose cosmopolitan air of not belonging to any town. One was clad in a suit of white canvas, another in a cap and blouse, the third in an old military frock, the fourth in a shapeless dress that looked as if it had been made out of old umbrellas. All wore dust-coloured shoes. My heart beat high; for, in those four male personages, although complexionless and eyebrowless, I beheld four subjects of the Family P. Salcy. Blue-bearded though they were, and bereft of the youthful smoothness of cheek which is imparted by what is termed in Albion a 'Whitechapel shave' (and which is, in fact, whitening, judiciously applied to the jaws with the palm of the hand), I recognised them. As I stood admiring, there emerged from the yard of a lowly Cabaret, the excellent Ma Mère, Ma Mère, with the words, 'The soup is served;' words which so elated the subject in the canvas suit, that when they all ran in to partake, he went last, dancing with his hands stuck angularly into the pockets of his canvas trousers, after the Pierrot manner. Glancing down the Yard, the last I saw of him was, that he looked in through a window (at the soup, no doubt) on one leg.

Full of this pleasure, I shortly afterwards departed from the town, little dreaming of an addition to my good fortune. But more was in reserve. I went by a train which was heavy with third-class carriages, full of young fellows (well guarded) who had drawn unlucky numbers in the last conscription, and were on their way to a famous French garrison town where much of the raw military material is worked up into soldiery. At the station they had been sitting about, in their threadbare homespun blue garments, with their poor little bundles under their arms, covered with dust and clay, and the various soils of France; sad enough at heart, most of them, but putting a good face upon it, and slapping their breasts and singing choruses on the smallest provocation; the gayer spirits shouldering half loaves of black bread speared upon their walking-sticks. As we went along, they were audible at every station, chorusing wildly out of tune, and feigning the highest hilarity. After a while, however, they began to leave off singing, and to laugh naturally, while at intervals there mingled with their laughter the barking of a dog. Now, I had to alight short of their destination, and as that stoppage of the train was attended with a quantity of horn blowing, bell ringing, and proclamation of what Messieurs les Voyageurs were to do, and were not to do, in order to reach their respective destinations, I had ample leisure to go forward on the platform to take a parting look at my recruits, whose heads were all out at window, and who were laughing like delighted children. Then I perceived that a large poodle with a pink nose, who had been their travelling companion and the cause of their mirth, stood on his hind-legs presenting arms on the extreme verge of the platform, ready to salute them as the train went off. This poodle wore a military shako (it is unnecessary to add, very much on one side over one eye), a little military coat, and the regulation white gaiters. He was armed with a little musket and a little sword-bayonet, and he stood presenting arms in perfect attitude, with his unobscured eye on his master or superior officer, who stood by him. So admirable was his discipline, that, when the train moved, and he was greeted with the parting cheers of the recruits, and also with a shower of centimes, several of which struck his shako, and had a tendency to discompose him, he remained staunch on his post, until the train was gone. He then resigned his arms to his officer, took off his shako by rubbing his paw over it, dropped on four legs, bringing his uniform coat into the absurdest relations with the overarching skies, and ran about the platform in his white gaiters, wagging his tail to an exceeding great extent. It struck me that there was more waggery than this in the poodle, and that he knew that the recruits would neither get through their exercises, nor get rid of their uniforms, as easily as he; revolving which in my thoughts, and seeking in my pockets some small money to bestow upon him, I casually directed my eyes to the face of his superior officer, and in him beheld the Face-Maker! Though it was not the way to Algeria, but quite the reverse, the military poodle's Colonel was the Face-Maker in a dark blouse, with a small bundle dangling over his shoulder at the end of an umbrella, and taking a pipe from his breast to smoke as he and the poodle went their mysterious way.

From his observations in provincial France, Dickens composed what he described as 'a complete Camera Obscura *of a dull little fortified French town', in the form of a story which he contributed, in collaboration with Wilkie Collins, to a kind of portmanteau called* Somebody's Luggage. *The original title of the story, 'His Boots', being inexplicable apart from that context, I have here altered it to 'Bebelle and the French Corporal'. Dickens really* did *see that soldier and that baby.*

BEBELLE AND THE FRENCH CORPORAL

'Eh! well then, Monsieur Mutuel! What do I know, what can I say? I assure you that he calls himself Monsieur The Englishman.'

'Pardon. But I think it is impossible,' said Monsieur Mutuel, – a spectacled, snuffy, stooping old gentleman in carpet shoes and a cloth cap with a peaked shade, a loose blue frock-coat reaching to his heels, a large limp white shirt-frill, and cravat to correspond, – that is to say, white was the natural colour of his linen on Sundays, but it toned down with the week.

'It is,' repeated Monsieur Mutuel, his amiable old walnut-shell countenance very walnut-shelly indeed as he smiled and blinked in the bright morning sunlight, – 'it is, my cherished Madame Bouclet, I think, impossible!'

'Hey!' (with a little vexed cry and a great many tosses of her head.) 'But it is not impossible that you are a Pig!' retorted Madame Bouclet, a compact little woman of thirty-five or so. 'See then, – look there, – read! "On the second floor Monsieur L'Anglais." Is it not so?'

'It is so,' said Monsieur Mutuel.

'Good. Continue your morning walk. Get out!' Madame Bouclet dismissed him with a lively snap of her fingers.

The morning walk of Monsieur Mutuel was in the brightest patch that the sun made in the Grande Place of a dull old fortified French town. The manner of his morning walk was with his hands crossed behind him; an umbrella, in figure the express image of himself, always in one hand; a snuff-box in the other. Thus, with the shuffling gait of the Elephant (who really does deal with the very worst trousers-maker employed by the Zoological world, and who appeared to have recommended him to Monsieur Mutuel), the old gentleman sunned himself daily when sun was to be had – of course, at the same time sunning a red ribbon at his button-hole; for was he not an ancient Frenchman?

Being told by one of the angelic sex to continue his morning walk and get out, Monsieur Mutuel laughed a walnut-shell laugh, pulled off his cap at arm's length with the hand that contained his snuff-box, kept it off for a considerable period after he had parted from Madame Bouclet, and continued his morning walk and got out, like a man of gallantry as he was.

The documentary evidence to which Madame Bouclet had referred Monsieur Mutuel was the list of her lodgers, sweetly written forth by her own Nephew and Bookkeeper, who held the pen of an Angel, and posted up at the side of her gateway, for the information of the Police: 'Au second, M. L'Anglais, Propriétaire.' On the second floor, Mr The Englishman, man of property. So it stood; nothing could be plainer.

Madame Bouclet now traced the line with her forefinger, as it were to confirm and settle herself in her parting snap at Monsieur Mutuel, and so placing her right hand on her hip with a defiant air, as if nothing should ever tempt her to unsnap that snap, strolled out into the Place to glance up at the windows of Mr The Englishman. That worthy happening to be looking out of window at the moment, Madame Bouclet gave him a graceful salutation with her head, looked to the right and looked to the left to account to him for her being there, considered for a moment, like one who accounted to herself for somebody she had expected not being there, and re-entered her own gateway. Madame Bouclet let all her house giving on the Place in furnished flats or floors, and lived up the yard behind in company with Monsieur Bouclet her husband (great at billiards), an inherited brewing business, several fowls, two carts, a nephew, a little dog in a big kennel, a grape-vine, a counting-house, four horses, a married sister (with a share in the brewing business), the husband and two children of the married sister, a parrot, a drum (performed on by the little boy of the married sister), two billeted soldiers, a quantity of pigeons, a fife (played by the nephew in a ravishing manner), several domestics and supernumeraries, a perpetual flavour of coffee and soup, a terrific range of artificial rocks and wooden precipices at least four feet high, a small fountain, and half-a-dozen large sunflowers.

Now the Englishman, in taking his Appartement, – or, as one might say on our side of the Channel, his set of chambers, – had given his name, correct to the letter, LANGLEY. But as he had a British way of not opening his mouth very wide on foreign soil, except at meals, the Brewery had been able to make nothing of it but L'Anglais. So Mr The Englishman he had become and he remained.

'Never saw such a people!' muttered Mr The Englishman, as he now looked out of window. 'Never did, in my life!'

This was true enough, for he had never before been out of his own country, – a right little island, a tight little island, a bright little island, a show-fight little island, and full of merit of all sorts; but not the whole round world.

'These chaps,' said Mr The Englishman to himself, as his eye rolled over the Place, sprinkled with military here and there, 'are no more like soldiers –' Nothing being sufficiently strong for the end of his sentence, he left it unended.

This again (from the point of view of his experience) was strictly correct; for though there was a great agglomeration of soldiers in the town and neighbouring country, you might have held a grand Review and Field-day of them every one, and looked in vain among them all for a soldier choking behind his foolish stock, or a soldier lamed by his ill-fitting shoes, or a soldier deprived of the use of his limbs by straps and buttons, or a soldier elaborately forced to be self-helpless in all the small affairs of life. A swarm of brisk, bright, active, bustling, handy, odd, skirmishing fellows, able to turn cleverly at anything, from a siege to soup, from great guns to needles and thread, from the broadsword exercise to slicing an onion, from making war to making omelets, was all you would have found.

What a swarm! From the Great Place under the eye of Mr The Englishman, where a few awkward squads from the last conscription were doing the goose-step – some members of those squads still as to their bodies, in the chrysalis peasant-state of Blouse, and only military butterflies as to their regimentally-clothed legs – from the Great Place, away outside the fortifications, and away for miles along the dusty roads, soldiers swarmed. All day long, upon the grass-grown ramparts of the town, practising soldiers trumpeted and bugled; all day long, down in angles of dry trenches, practising soldiers drummed and drummed. Every forenoon, soldiers burst out of the great barracks into the sandy gymnasium-ground hard by, and flew over the wooden horse, and hung on to flying ropes, and dangled upside-down between parallel bars, and shot themselves off wooden platforms, – splashes, sparks, coruscations, showers of soldiers. At every corner of the town-wall, every guard-house, every gateway, every sentry-box, every drawbridge, every reedy ditch, and rushy dike, soldiers, soldiers, soldiers. And the town being pretty well all wall, guard-house, gateway, sentry-box, drawbridge, reedy ditch, and rushy dike, the town was pretty well all soldiers.

What would the sleepy old town have been without the soldiers, seeing that even with them it had so overslept itself as to have slept its echoes hoarse, its defensive bars and locks and bolts and chains all rusty, and its ditches stagnant! From the days when VAUBAN engineered it to that perplexing extent that to look at it was like being knocked on the head with it, the stranger becoming stunned and stertorous under the shock of its incomprehensibility, – from the days when VAUBAN made it the express incorporation of every substantive and adjective in the art of military engineering, and not only twisted you into it and twisted you out of it, to the right, to the left, opposite, under here, over there, in the dark, in the dirt, by the gateway, archway, covered way, dry way, wet way, fosse, portcullis, drawbridge, sluice, squat tower, pierced wall, and heavy battery, but likewise took a fortifying dive under the neighbouring country, and came to the surface three or four miles off, blowing out incomprehensible mounds and batteries among the quiet crops of chicory and beet-root, – from those days to these the town had been asleep, and dust and rust and must had settled on its drowsy Arsenals and Magazines, and grass had grown up in its silent streets.

On market-days alone, its Great Place suddenly leaped out of bed. On market-days, some friendly enchanter struck his staff upon the stones of the Great Place, and instantly arose the liveliest booths and stalls, and sittings and standings, and a pleasant hum of chaffering and huckstering from many hundreds of tongues, and a pleasant, though peculiar, blending of colours, – white caps, blue blouses, and green vegetables, – and at last the Knight destined for the adventure seemed to have come in earnest, and all the Vaubanois sprang up awake. And now, by long, low-lying avenues of trees, jolting in white-hooded donkey-cart, and on donkey-back, and in tumbril and wagon, and cart and cabriolet, and afoot with barrow and burden, – and along the dikes and ditches and canals, in little peak-prowed country boats, – came peasant-men and women in flocks and crowds, bringing articles for sale. And here you had boots and shoes, and sweetmeats and stuffs to wear, and here (in the cool shade of the Town-hall) you had milk and cream and butter and cheese, and here you had fruits and onions and carrots, and all things needful for your soup, and here you had poultry and flowers and protesting pigs, and here new shovels, axes, spades, and bill-hooks for your farming work, and here huge mounds of bread, and here your unground grain in sacks, and here your children's dolls, and here the cake-seller, announcing his wares by beat and roll of drum. And hark! fanfaronade of trumpets, and here into the Great Place, resplendent in an open carriage, with four gorgeously-attired servitors up behind, playing horns, drums, and cymbals, rolled 'the Daughter of a Physician' in massive golden chains and earrings, and blue-feathered hat, shaded from the admiring sun by two immense umbrellas of artificial roses, to dispense (from motives of philanthropy) that small and pleasant dose which had cured so many thousands! Toothache, earache, headache, heartache, stomachache, debility, nervousness, fits, fainting, fever, ague, all equally cured by the small and pleasant dose of the great Physician's great daughter! The process was this, – she, the Daughter of a Physician, proprietress of the superb equipage you now admired with its confirmatory blasts of trumpet, drum, and cymbal, told you so: On the first day after taking the small and pleasant dose, you would feel no particular influence beyond a most harmonious sensation of indescribable and irresistible joy; on the second day you would be so astonishingly better that you would think yourself changed into somebody else; on the third day you would be entirely free from your disorder, whatever its nature and however long you had had it, and would seek out the Physician's Daughter to throw yourself at her feet, kiss the hem of her garment, and buy as many more of the small and pleasant doses as by the sale of all your few effects you could obtain; but she would be inaccessible, – gone for herbs to the Pyramids of Egypt, – and you would be (though cured) reduced to despair! Thus would the Physician's Daughter drive her trade (and briskly too), and thus would the buying and selling and mingling of tongues and colours continue, until the changing sunlight, leaving the Physician's Daughter in the shadow of high roofs, admonished her to jolt out westward, with a departing effect of gleam and glitter on the splendid equipage and brazen blast. And now the enchanter struck his staff upon the stones of the Great Place once more, and down went the booths, the sittings and standings, and vanished the merchandise, and with it the barrows, donkeys, donkey-carts, and tumbrils, and all other things on wheels and feet, except the slow scavengers with unwieldy carts and meagre horses clearing up the rubbish, assisted by the sleek town pigeons, better plumped out than on non-market days. While there was yet an hour or two to wane before the autumn sunset, the loiterer outside town-gate and drawbridge, and postern and double-ditch, would see the last white-hooded cart lessening in the avenue of lengthening shadows of trees, or the last country boat, paddled by the last market-woman on her way home, showing black upon the reddening, long, low, narrow dike between him and the mill; and as the paddle-parted scum and weed closed over the boat's track, he might be comfortably sure that its sluggish rest would be troubled no more until next market-day.

As it was not one of the Great Place's days for getting out of bed, when Mr The Englishman looked down at the young soldiers practising the goose-step there, his mind was left at liberty to take a military turn.

'These fellows are billeted everywhere about,' said he; 'and to see them lighting the people's fires, boiling the people's pots, minding the people's babies, rocking the people's cradles, washing the people's greens, and making themselves generally useful, in every sort of unmilitary way, is most ridiculous! Never saw such a set of fellows, – never did in my life!'

All perfectly true again. Was there not Private Valentine in that very house, acting as sole housemaid, valet, cook, steward, and nurse, in the family of his captain, Monsieur le Capitaine de la Cour, – cleaning the floors, making the beds, doing the marketing, dressing the captain, dressing the dinners, dressing the salads, and dressing the baby, all with equal readiness? Or, to put him aside, he being in loyal attendance on his Chief, was there not Private Hyppolite, billeted at the Perfumer's two hundred yards off, who, when not on duty, volunteered to keep shop while the fair Perfumeress stepped out to speak to a neighbour or so, and laughingly sold soap with his war-sword girded on him? Was there not Emile, billeted at the Clock-maker's, perpetually turning to of an evening, with his coat off, winding up the stock? Was there not Eugène, billeted at the Tinman's, cultivating, pipe in mouth, a garden four feet square, for the Tinman, in the little court, behind the shop, and extorting the fruits of the earth from the same, on his knees, with the sweat of his brow? Not to multiply examples, was there not Baptiste, billeted on the poor Water-carrier, at that very instant sitting on the pavement in the sunlight, with his martial legs asunder, and one of the Water-carrier's spare pails between them, which (to the delight and glory of the heart of the Water-carrier coming across the Place from the fountain, yoked and burdened) he was painting bright-green outside and bright-red within? Or, to go no farther than the Barber's at the very next door, was there not Corporal Théophile——

'No,' said Mr The Englishman, glancing down at the Barber's, 'he is not there at present. There's the child, though.'

A mere mite of a girl stood on the steps of the Barber's shop, looking across the Place. A mere baby, one might call her, dressed in the close white linen cap which small French country children wear (like the children in Dutch pictures), and in a frock of homespun blue, that had no shape except where it was tied round her little fat throat. So that, being naturally short and round all over, she looked, behind, as if she had been cut off at her natural waist, and had had her head neatly fitted on it.

'There's the child, though.'

To judge from the way in which the dimpled hand was rubbing the eyes, the eyes had been closed in a nap, and were newly opened. But they seemed to be looking so intently across the Place, that the Englishman looked in the same direction.

'O!' said he presently. 'I thought as much. The Corporal's there.'

The Corporal, a smart figure of a man of thirty, perhaps a thought under the middle size, but very neatly made, – a sunburnt Corporal with a brown peaked beard, – faced about at the moment, addressing voluble words of instruction to the squad in hand. Nothing was amiss or awry about the Corporal. A lithe and nimble Corporal, quite complete, from the sparkling dark eyes under his knowing uniform cap to his sparkling white gaiters. The very image and presentment of a Corporal of his country's army, in the line of his shoulders, the line of his waist, the broadest line of his Bloomer trousers, and their narrowest line at the calf of his leg.

Mr The Englishman looked on, and the child looked on, and the Corporal looked on (but the last-named at his men), until the drill ended a few minutes afterwards, and the military sprinkling dried up directly, and was gone. Then said Mr The Englishman to himself, 'Look here! By George!' And the Corporal, dancing towards the Barber's with his arms wide open, caught up the child, held her over his head in a flying attitude, caught her down again, kissed her, and made off with her into the Barber's house.

Now Mr The Englishman had had a quarrel with his erring and disobedient and disowned daughter, and there was a child in that case too. Had not his daughter been a child, and had she not taken angel-flights above his head as this child had flown above the Corporal's?

'He's a' – National Participled – 'fool!' said the Englishman, and shut his window.

But the windows of the house of Memory, and the windows of the house of Mercy, are not so easily closed as windows of glass and wood. They fly open unexpectedly; they rattle in the night; they must be nailed up. Mr The Englishman had tried nailing them, but had not driven the nails quite home. So he passed but a disturbed evening and a worse night.

By nature a good-tempered man? No; very little gentleness, confounding the quality with weakness. Fierce and wrathful when crossed? Very, and stupendously unreasonable. Moody? Exceedingly so. Vindictive? Well; he *had* had scowling thoughts that he would formally curse his daughter, as he had seen it done on the stage. But remembering that the real Heaven is some paces removed from the mock one in the great chandelier of the Theatre, he had given that up.

And he had come abroad to be rid of his repudiated daughter for the rest of his life. And here he was.

At bottom, it was for this reason, more than for any other, that Mr The Englishman took it extremely ill that Corporal Théophile should be so devoted to little Bebelle, the child at the Barber's shop. In an unlucky moment he had chanced to say to himself, 'Why, confound the fellow, he is not her father!' There was a sharp sting in the speech which ran into him suddenly, and put him in a worse mood. So he had National Participled the unconscious Corporal with most hearty emphasis, and had made up his mind to think no more about such a mountebank.

But it came to pass that the Corporal was not to be dismissed. If he had known the most delicate fibres of the Englishman's mind, instead of knowing nothing on earth about him, and if he had been the most obstinate Corporal in the Grand Army of France, instead of being the most obliging, he could not have planted himself with more determined immovability plumb in the midst of all the Englishman's thoughts. Not only so, but he seemed to be always in his view. Mr The Englishman had but to look out of window, to look upon the Corporal with little Bebelle. He had but to go for a walk, and there was the Corporal walking with Bebelle. He had but to come home again, disgusted, and the Corporal and Bebelle were at home before him. If he looked out at his back windows early in the morning, the Corporal was in the Barber's back yard, washing and dressing and brushing Bebelle. If he took refuge at his front windows, the Corporal brought his breakfast out into the Place, and shared it there with Bebelle. Always Corporal and always Bebelle. Never Corporal without Bebelle. Never Bebelle without Corporal.

Mr The Englishman was not particularly strong in the French language as a means of oral communication, though he read it very well. It is with languages as with people, – when you only know them by sight, you are apt to mistake them; you must be on speaking terms before you can be said to have established an acquaintance.

For this reason, Mr The Englishman had to gird up his loins considerably before he could bring himself to the point of exchanging ideas with Madame Bouclet on the subject of this Corporal and this Bebelle. But Madame Bouclet looking in apologetically one morning to remark, that, O Heaven! she was in a state of desolation because the lamp-maker had not sent home that lamp confided to him to repair, but that truly he was a lamp-maker against whom the whole world shrieked out, Mr The Englishman seized the occasion.

'Madame, that baby——'

'Pardon, monsieur. That lamp.'

'No, no, that little girl.'

'But, pardon!' said Madame Bouclet, angling for a clew, 'one cannot light a little girl, or send her to be repaired?'

'The little girl – at the house of the barber.'

'Ah-h-h!' cried Madame Bouclet, suddenly catching the idea with her delicate little line and rod. 'Little Bebelle? Yes, yes, yes! And her friend the Corporal? Yes, yes, yes, yes! So genteel of him, – is it not?'

'He is not——?'

'Not at all; not at all! He is not one of her relations. Not at all!'

'Why, then, he——'

'Perfectly!' cried Madame Bouclet, 'you are right, monsieur. It is so genteel of him. The less relation, the more genteel. As you say.'

'Is she——?'

'The child of the barber?' Madame Bouclet whisked up her skilful little line and rod again. 'Not at all, not at all! She is the child of – in a word, of no one.'

'The wife of the barber, then——?'

'Indubitably. As you say. The wife of the barber receives a small stipend to take care of her. So much by the month. Eh, then! It is without doubt very little, for we are all poor here.'

'You are not poor, madame.'

'As to my lodgers,' replied Madame Bouclet, with a smiling and a gracious bend of her head, 'no. As to all things else, so-so.'

'You flatter me, madame.'

'Monsieur, it is you who flatter me in living here.'

Certain fishy gasps on Mr The Englishman's part, denoting that he was about to resume his subject under difficulties,

Madame Bouclet observed him closely, and whisked up her delicate line and rod again with triumphant success.

'O no, monsieur, certainly not. The wife of the barber is not cruel to the poor child, but she is careless. Her health is delicate, and she sits all day, looking out at window. Consequently, when the Corporal first came, the poor little Bebelle was much neglected.'

'It is a curious——' began Mr The Englishman.

'Name? That Bebelle? Again you are right, monsieur. But it is a playful name for Gabrielle.'

'And so the child is a mere fancy of the Corporal's?' said Mr The Englishman, in a gruffly disparaging tone of voice.

'Eh, well!' returned Madame Bouclet, with a pleading shrug: 'one must love something. Human nature is weak.'

('Devilish weak,' muttered the Englishman, in his own language.)

'And the Corporal,' pursued Madame Bouclet, 'being billeted at the barber's, – where he will probably remain a long time, for he is attached to the General, – and finding the poor unowned child in need of being loved, and finding himself in need of loving, – why, there you have it all, you see!'

Mr The Englishman accepted this interpretation of the matter with an indifferent grace, and observed to himself, in an injured manner, when he was again alone: 'I shouldn't mind it so much, if these people were not such a' – National Participled – 'sentimental people!'

There was a Cemetery outside the town, and it happened ill for the reputation of the Vaubanois, in this sentimental connexion, that he took a walk there that same afternoon. To be sure there were some wonderful things in it (from the Englishman's point of view), and of a certainty in all Britain you would have found nothing like it. Not to mention the fanciful flourishes of hearts and crosses in wood and iron, that were planted all over the place, making it look very like a Firework-ground, where a most splendid pyrotechnic display might be expected after dark, there were so many wreaths upon the graves, embroidered, as it might be, 'To my mother,' 'To my daughter,' 'To my father,'

'To my brother,' 'To my sister,' 'To my friend,' and those many wreaths were in so many stages of elaboration and decay, from the wreath of yesterday, all fresh colour and bright beads, to the wreath of last year, a poor mouldering wisp of straw! There were so many little gardens and grottoes made upon graves, in so many tastes, with plants and shells and plaster figures and porcelain pitchers, and so many odds and ends! There were so many tributes of remembrance hanging up, not to be discriminated by the closest inspection from little round waiters, whereon were depicted in glowing hues either a lady or a gentleman with a white pocket-handkerchief out of all proportion, leaning, in a state of the most faultless mourning and most profound affliction, on the most architectural and gorgeous urn! There were so many surviving wives who had put their names on the tombs of their deceased husbands, with a blank for the date of their own departure from this weary world; and there were so many surviving husbands who had rendered the same homage to their deceased wives; and out of the number there must have been so many who had long ago married again! In fine, there was so much in the place that would have seemed mere frippery to a stranger, save for the consideration that the lightest paper flower that lay upon the poorest heap of earth was never touched by a rude hand, but perished there, a sacred thing!

'Nothing of the solemnity of Death here,' Mr The Englishman had been going to say, when this last consideration touched him with a mild appeal, and on the whole he walked out without saying it. 'But these people are,' he insisted, by way of compensation, when he was well outside the gate, 'they are so' – Participled – 'sentimental!'

His way back lay by the military gymnasium-ground. And there he passed the Corporal glibly instructing young soldiers how to swing themselves over rapid and deep water-courses on their way to Glory, by means of a rope, and himself deftly plunging off a platform, and flying a hundred feet or two, as an encouragement to them to begin. And there he also passed, perched on a crowning eminence (probably by the Corporal's careful hands), the small Bebelle, with her round eyes wide open, surveying the proceeding like a wondering sort of blue and white bird.

'If that child was to die,' this was his reflection as he turned his back and went his way, – 'and it would almost serve the fellow right for making such a fool of himself, – I suppose we should have *him* sticking up a wreath and a waiter in that fantastic burying-ground.'

Nevertheless, after another early morning or two of looking out of window, he strolled down into the Place, when the Corporal and Bebelle were walking there, and touching his hat to the Corporal (an immense achievement), wished him Good-day.

'Good-day, monsieur.'

'This is a rather pretty child you have here,' said Mr The Englishman, taking her chin in his hand, and looking down into her astonished blue eyes.

'Monsieur, she is a very pretty child,' returned the Corporal, with a stress on his polite correction of the phrase.

'And good?' said the Englishman.

'And very good. Poor little thing!'

'Hah!' The Englishman stooped down and patted her cheek, not without awkwardness, as if he were going too far in his conciliation. 'And what is this medal round your neck, my little one?'

Bebelle having no other reply on her lips than her chubby right fist, the Corporal offered his services as interpreter.

'Monsieur demands, what is this, Bebelle?'

'It is the Holy Virgin,' said Bebelle.

'And who gave it you?' asked the Englishman.

'Théophile.'

'And who is Théophile?'

Bebelle broke into a laugh, laughed merrily and heartily, clapped her chubby hands, and beat her little feet on the stone pavement of the Place.

'He doesn't know Théophile! Why, he doesn't know any one! He doesn't know anything!' Then, sensible of a small solecism in her manners, Bebelle twisted her right hand in a leg of the

Corporal's Bloomer trousers, and, laying her cheek against the place, kissed it.

'Monsieur Théophile, I believe?' said the Englishman to the Corporal.

'It is I, monsieur.'

'Permit me.' Mr The Englishman shook him heartily by the hand and turned away. But he took it mighty ill that old Monsieur Mutuel in his patch of sunlight, upon whom he came as he turned, should pull off his cap to him with a look of pleased approval. And he muttered, in his own tongue, as he returned the salutation, 'Well, walnut-shell! And what business is it of *yours*?'

Mr The Englishman went on for many weeks passing but disturbed evenings and worse nights, and constantly experiencing that those aforesaid windows in the houses of Memory and Mercy rattled after dark, and that he had very imperfectly nailed them up. Likewise, he went on for many weeks daily improving the acquaintance of the Corporal and Bebelle. That is to say, he took Bebelle by the chin, and the Corporal by the hand, and offered Bebelle sous and the Corporal cigars, and even got the length of changing pipes with the Corporal and kissing Bebelle. But he did it all in a shamefaced way, and always took it extremely ill that Monsieur Mutuel in his patch of sunlight should note what he did. Whenever that seemed to be the case, he always growled in his own tongue, 'There you are again, walnut-shell! What business is it of *yours*?'

In a word, it had become the occupation of Mr The Englishman's life to look after the Corporal and little Bebelle, and to resent old Monsieur Mutuel's looking after *him*. An occupation only varied by a fire in the town one windy night, and much passing of water-buckets from hand to hand (in which the Englishman rendered good service), and much beating of drums, – when all of a sudden the Corporal disappeared.

Next, all of a sudden, Bebelle disappeared.

She had been visible a few days later than the Corporal, – sadly deteriorated as to washing and brushing, – but she had not spoken when addressed by Mr The Englishman, and had looked scared and had run away. And now it would seem that she had run away for good. And there lay the Great Place under the windows, bare and barren.

In his shamefaced and constrained way, Mr The Englishman asked no question of any one, but watched from his front windows and watched from his back windows, and lingered about the Place, and peeped in at the Barber's shop, and did all this and much more with a whistling and tune-humming pretence of not missing anything, until one afternoon when Monsieur Mutuel's patch of sunlight was in shadow, and when, according to all rule and precedent, he had no right whatever to bring his red ribbon out of doors, behold here he was, advancing with his cap already in his hand twelve paces off!

Mr The Englishman had got as far into his usual objurgation as, 'What bu – si –' when he checked himself.

'Ah, it is sad, it is sad! Hélas, it is unhappy, it is sad!' Thus old Monsieur Mutuel, shaking his grey head.

'What busin – at least, I would say, what do you mean, Monsieur Mutuel?'

'Our Corporal. Hélas, our dear Corporal!'

'What has happened to him?'

'You have not heard?'

'No.'

'At the fire. But he was so brave, so ready. Ah, too brave, too ready!'

'May the Devil carry you away!' the Englishman broke in impatiently; 'I beg your pardon, – I mean me, – I am not accustomed to speak French, – go on, will you?'

'And a falling beam——'

'Good God!' exclaimed the Englishman. 'It was a private soldier who was killed?'

'No. A Corporal, the same Corporal, our dear Corporal. Beloved by all his comrades. The funeral ceremony was touching, – penetrating. Monsieur The Englishman, your eyes fill with tears.'

'What bu – si——'

'Monsieur The Englishman, I honour those emotions. I salute

you with profound respect. I will not obtrude myself upon your noble heart.'

Monsieur Mutuel, – a gentleman in every thread of his cloudy linen, under whose wrinkled hand every grain in the quarter of an ounce of poor snuff in his poor little tin box became a gentleman's property, – Monsieur Mutuel passed on, with his cap in his hand.

'I little thought,' said the Englishman, after walking for several minutes, and more than once blowing his nose, 'when I was looking round that cemetery – I'll go there!'

Straight he went there, and when he came within the gate he paused, considering whether he should ask at the lodge for some direction to the grave. But he was less than ever in a mood for asking questions, and he thought, 'I shall see something on it to know it by.'

In search of the Corporal's grave he went softly on, up this walk and down that, peering in, among the crosses and hearts and columns and obelisks and tombstones, for a recently disturbed spot. It troubled him now to think how many dead there were in the cemetery, – he had not thought them a tenth part so numerous before, – and after he had walked and sought for some time, he said to himself, as he struck down a new vista of tombs, 'I might suppose that every one was dead but I.'

Not every one. A live child was lying on the ground asleep. Truly he had found something on the Corporal's grave to know it by, and the something was Bebelle.

With such a loving will had the dead soldier's comrades worked at his resting-place, that it was already a neat garden. On the green turf of the garden Bebelle lay sleeping, with her cheek touching it. A plain, unpainted little wooden Cross was planted in the turf, and her short arm embraced this little Cross, as it had many a time embraced the Corporal's neck. They had put a tiny flag (the flag of France) at his head, and a laurel garland.

Mr The Englishman took off his hat, and stood for a while silent. Then, covering his head again, he bent down on one knee, and softly roused the child.

'Bebelle! My little one!'

Opening her eyes, on which the tears were still wet, Bebelle was at first frightened; but seeing who it was, she suffered him to take her in his arms, looking steadfastly at him.

'You must not lie here, my little one. You must come with me.'

'No, no. I can't leave Théophile. I want the good dear Théophile.'

'We will go and seek him, Bebelle. We will go and look for him in England. We will go and look for him at my daughter's, Bebelle.'

'Shall we find him there?'

'We shall find the best part of him there. Come with me, poor forlorn little one. Heaven is my witness,' said the Englishman, in a low voice, as, before he rose, he touched the turf above the gentle Corporal's breast, 'that I thankfully accept this trust!'

It was a long way for the child to have come unaided. She was soon asleep again, with her embrace transferred to the Englishman's neck. He looked at her worn shoes, and her galled feet, and her tired face, and believed that she had come there every day.

He was leaving the grave with the slumbering Bebelle in his arms, when he stopped, looked wistfully down at it, and looked wistfully at the other graves around. 'It is the innocent custom of the people,' said Mr The Englishman, with hesitation. 'I think I should like to do it. No one sees.'

Careful not to wake Bebelle as he went, he repaired to the lodge where such little tokens of remembrance were sold, and bought two wreaths. One, blue and white and glistening silver, 'To my friend;' one of a soberer red and black and yellow, 'To my friend.' With these he went back to the grave, and so down on one knee again. Touching the child's lips with the brighter wreath, he guided her hand to hang it on the Cross; then hung his own wreath there. After all, the wreaths were not far out of keeping with the little garden. To my friend. To my friend.

Mr The Englishman took it very ill when he looked round a street corner into the Great Place, carrying Bebelle in his arms, that old Mutuel should be there airing his red ribbon. He took a world of pains to dodge the worthy Mutuel, and devoted a surprising amount of time and trouble to skulking into his own lodging like a man pursued by Justice. Safely arrived there at last, he made Bebelle's toilet with as accurate a remembrance as he could bring to bear upon that work of the way in which he had often seen the poor Corporal make it, and having given her to eat and drink, laid her down on his own bed. Then he slipped out into the Barber's shop, and after a brief interview with the Barber's wife, and a brief recourse to his purse and card-case, came back again with the whole of Bebelle's personal property in such a very little bundle that it was quite lost under his arm.

As it was irreconcilable with his whole course and character that he should carry Bebelle off in state, or receive any compliments or congratulations on that feat, he devoted the next day to getting his two portmanteaus out of the house by artfulness and stealth, and to comporting himself in every particular as if he were going to run away, – except, indeed, that he paid his few debts in the town, and prepared a letter to leave for Madame Bouclet, enclosing a sufficient sum of money in lieu of notice. A railway train would come through at midnight, and by that train he would take away Bebelle to look for Théophile in England and at his forgiven daughter's.

At midnight, on a moonlight night, Mr The Englishman came creeping forth like a harmless assassin, with Bebelle on his breast instead of a dagger. Quiet the Great Place, and quiet the never-stirring streets; closed the cafés; huddled together motionless their billiard-balls; drowsy the guard or sentinel on duty here and there; lulled for the time, by sleep, even the insatiate appetite of the Office of Town-dues.

Mr The Englishman left the Place behind, and left the streets behind, and left the civilian-inhabited town behind, and descended down among the military works of Vauban, hemming all in. As the shadow of the first heavy arch and postern fell upon him and was left behind, as the shadow of the second heavy arch and postern fell upon him and was left behind, as his hollow tramp over the first drawbridge was succeeded by a gentler sound, as his hollow tramp over the second drawbridge was succeeded by a gentler sound, as he overcame the stagnant ditches one by one, and passed out where the flowing waters were and where the moonlight, so the dark shades and the hollow sounds and the unwholesomely locked currents of his soul were vanquished and set free. See to it, Vaubans of your own hearts, who gird them in with triple walls and ditches, and with bolt and chain and bar and lifted bridge, – raze those fortifications, and lay them level with the all-absorbing dust, before the night cometh when no hand can work!

All went prosperously, and he got into an empty carriage in the train, where he could lay Bebelle on the seat over against him, as on a couch, and cover her from head to foot with his mantle. He had just drawn himself up from perfecting this arrangement, and had just leaned back in his own seat contemplating it with great satisfaction, when he became aware of a curious appearance at the open carriage window, – a ghostly little tin box floating up in the moonlight, and hovering there.

He leaned forward, and put out his head. Down among the rails and wheels and ashes, Monsieur Mutuel, red ribbon and all!

'Excuse me, Monsieur The Englishman,' said Monsieur Mutuel, holding up his box at arm's length, the carriage being so high and he so low; 'but I shall reverence the little box for ever, if your so generous hand will take a pinch from it at parting.'

Mr The Englishman reached out of the window before complying, and – without asking the old fellow what business it was of his – shook hands and said, 'Adieu! God bless you!'

'And, Mr The Englishman, God bless *you*!' cried Madame Bouclet, who was also there among the rails and wheels and ashes. 'And God will bless you in the happiness of the protected child now with you. And God will bless you in your own child at home. And God will bless you in your own remembrances. And this from me!'

He had barely time to catch a bouquet from her hand, when the train was flying through the night. Round the paper that enfolded it was bravely written (doubtless by the nephew who held the pen of an Angel), 'Homage to the friend of the friendless.'

'Not bad people, Bebelle!' said Mr The Englishman, softly drawing the mantle a little from her sleeping face that he might kiss it, 'though they are so——'

Too 'sentimental' himself at the moment to be able to get out that word, he added nothing but a sob, and travelled for some miles, through the moonlight, with his hand before his eyes.

Switzerland and Italy

From Boulogne, on 27 August 1853, Dickens sent to a friend his proposed itinerary for the holiday he spent, it later proved, in company with Wilkie Collins and the artist Augustus Egg.

I contemplate starting from here on Monday, the tenth of October. I shall first go by Paris and Geneva to Lausanne, for it has a special place in my memory. If the autumn should be very fine (just possible after such a summer) I shall then go by Chamonix and Martigny over the Simplon to Milan, thence to Genoa, Leghorn, Pisa and Naples, thence I hope to Sicily. Back to Bologna, Florence, Rome, Verona, Mantua, etc., to Venice, and home by Germany, arriving in good time for Christmas Day.

Except for Sicily, all this befell (trust Dickens!) pretty well as planned, and was recorded in many amusing and some serious letters. For Dickens it was so often a re-tracing and recollection of old scenes and meeting with old friends, and for Collins and Egg a great new adventure.

There were no more Pictures from Italy, *but as soon as Dickens got back to work he started writing* Little Dorrit, *the only one of his novels to be involved with his experiences in Europe. Many passages, not unexpectedly, read like revised versions of his* Pictures, *but they are skilfully woven into the story.*

The very first pages transport the reader from the unbearable white glare of Marseilles scorching in the sun into the hateful prison (of which Dickens had seen so many) which the villain Rigaud shares with the charming little Italian, Jean Baptiste Cavelletto, who is to reappear at intervals like a shaft of sunshine in gloomy places.

How often had Dickens seen 'that peculiar shake of the right hand which is the most expressive negative in the Italian language'; how often had he heard that one word 'Altro'.

'Altro', returned John Baptist, closing his eyes and giving his head a most vehement toss. The word being, according to the Genoese emphasis, a confirmation, a contradiction, an assertion, a denial, a taunt, a complaint, a joke, and fifty other things, became in the present instance with a significance beyond all power of written expression, our familiar English 'I believe you'.

When Jean Baptist finds himself living among the working people of London in Bleeding Heart Yard, his co-tenant, Mrs Plornish, invents her own English-Italian, 'Me 'ope you leg better?', which she is convinced he is bound to understand if only she speaks loudly enough. And the kindly patronage of all those indigent neighbours towards the poor little man who is so unfortunate as not to be English is in essence just the same as the attitude of Mr Meagles, the affluent traveller who 'addresses individuals of all nations in idiomatic English with a perfect conviction that they were bound to understand it somehow'.

And this was the kind of address which Dickens had noticed was so generally used by his own servants when they had first arrived in Genoa. Except for Venice, where he and his two friends stayed for a thrilling few days, Genoa was the place that he most wanted to revisit. The changes he found were on the whole for the better, but, he told Forster, the Peschiere had been converted into a girls' school and all the paintings of gods and goddesses 'canvassed over'. But the old familiar smell as of 'very rotten cheese kept in very hot blankets' was still prevalent in some well-remembered places; the man without legs was still in the Strada Nuova, but the beggars in general had 'all cleared off'. His old feelings about Genoa came back with a rush. 'Oh, what a wonderful place!'

Towards the end of that holiday, Dickens wrote to Forster:

I am more than ever confirmed in my conviction that one of the greatest uses of travelling is to encourage a man to think for himself, to be bold enough always to declare without offence that he *does* think for himself.

In Italy there was always plenty to think about. In 1848 Mazzini had been released from exile and, on going to Rome, had found to his surprise that a popular revolution had taken place and that the Pope had fled. In the following year Mazzini had become one of the triumvirate who were to govern Rome for nine months. But the other states would not, or could not, co-operate, and the old foreign oppression came back with more force than ever. Now, in 1853, Dickens found the Austrians all over the place. But, 'thinking for himself', he had to admit that, greatly as he detested their treatment of the Italians, he found that their attitude towards travellers like himself was courteous and efficient, and that often, when trouble arose, it was the English who were to blame.

TURIN

This is a remarkably agreeable place. A beautiful town, prosperous, thriving, growing prodigiously, as Genoa is; crowded with busy inhabitants; full of noble streets and squares. The Alps, now covered deep with snow, are close upon it, and here and there seem almost ready to tumble into the houses. The contrast this part of Italy presents to the rest, is amazing. Beautifully made railroads, admirably managed; cheerful, active people; spirit, energy, life, progress. In Milan, in every street, the noble palace of some exile is a barrack, and dirty soldiers are lolling out of the magnificent windows – it seems as if the whole place were being gradually absorbed into soldiers. In Naples, something like a hundred thousand troops. 'I knew,' I said to a certain Neapolitan Marchese there whom I had known before, and who came to see me the night after I arrived, 'I knew a very remarkable gentleman when I was last here; who had never been out of his own country, but was perfectly acquainted with English literature, and had taught himself to speak English in that wonderful manner that no one could have known him for a foreigner; I am very anxious to see him again; but I forget his name.' – He named him, and his face fell directly. 'Dead?' said I. – 'In exile.' – 'O dear me!' said I, 'I had looked forward to seeing him again, more than anyone I was acquainted with in the country!' – 'What would you have?' says the Marchese in a low voice. 'He was a remarkable man – full of knowledge, full of spirit, full of generosity. Where should he be but in exile! Where could he be!' We said not another word about it, but I shall always remember the short dialogue.

I am strongly inclined to think that our countrymen are to blame in the matter of the Austrian vexations to travellers that have been complained of. Their manner is so very bad, they are so extraordinarily suspicious, so determined to be done by everybody, and give so much offence. Now, the Austrian police are very strict, but they really know how to do business, and they do it. And if you treat them like gentlemen, they will always respond. When we first crossed the Austrian frontier, and were ushered into the police office, I took off my hat. The officer immediately took off his, and was as polite – still doing his duty, without any compromise – as it was possible to be. When we came to Venice, the arrangements were very strict, but were so business-like that the smallest possible amount of inconvenience consistent with strictness ensued. Here is the scene. A soldier has come into the railway carriage (a saloon on the American plan) some miles off, has touched his hat, and asked for my passport. I have given it. Soldier has touched his hat again, and retired as from the presence of a superior officer. Alighted from carriage, we pass into a place like a banking-house, lighted up with gas. Nobody bullies us or drives us there, but we must go, because the road ends there. Several soldierly clerks. One very sharp chief. My passport is brought out of an inner room, certified to be *en règle*. Very sharp chief takes it, looks at it (it is rather longer, now, than *Hamlet*), calls out – 'Signor Carlo Dickens!' 'Here I am sir.' 'Do you intend remaining long in Venice sir?' 'Probably four days sir!' 'Italian is known to you sir. You have been in Venice before?' 'Once before sir.' 'Perhaps you remained longer then sir?' 'No indeed; I merely came to see, and went as I came.' 'Truly sir? Do I infer that you are going by Trieste?' 'No. I am going to Parma, and Turin, and by Paris home.' 'A cold journey sir, I hope it may be a pleasant one.' 'Thank you.' – He gives me one very sharp look all over, and wishes me a very happy night. I wish *him* a very happy night and it's done. The thing being done at all, could not be better done, or more politely – though I dare say if I had been sucking a gentish cane all the time, or talking in English to my compatriots, it might not unnaturally have been different. At Turin and at Genoa there are no such stoppages at all; but in any other part of Italy, give me an Austrian in preference to a native functionary. At Naples it is done in a beggarly, shambling, bungling, tardy, vulgar way; but I am strengthened in my old impression that Naples is one of the most odious places on the face of the earth. The general degradation oppresses me like foul air.

But, to end his Italian saga on a more typically cheerful note, here is another view of Dickens' Naples, where, indeed, he spent many hours with congenial friends, including the distinguished archaeologist, Layard, with whom he made his second ascent of Vesuvius. On 13 November, from Rome, he wrote to Georgina, looking back upon a ludicrous little adventure.

FANTASY IN NAPLES

One night, at Naples, Edward [the courier] came in, open-mouthed, to the table d'hote where we were dining with the Tennents, to announce 'The Marchese Garofolo'. I at first thought it must be the little parrot-marquess who was once your excort from Genoa; but I found him to be a man (married to an Englishwoman) whom we used to meet at Ridgeways. He was very glad to see me, and I afterwards met him at dinner at Mr Lowther's, our chargé d'affaires . . . We had an exceedingly pleasant dinner of eight, preparatory to which I was near having the ridiculous adventure of not being able to find the house and coming back dinnerless. I went in an open carriage from the hotel in all state, and the coachman, to my surprise, pulled up at the end of the Chiaja. 'Behold the house', says he, 'of Il Signor Larthoor!' – at the same time pointing with his whip into the seventh heaven, where the early stars were shining. 'But the Signor Larthoor', returns the Inimitable darling, 'lives at Pausilippo'. 'It is true', says the coachman (still pointing to the evening star) 'but he lives high up the Salita Sant' Antonio, where no carriage ever yet ascended and that is the house' (evening star as aforesaid), 'and one must go on foot. Behold the Salita Sant' Antonio!' I went up it, a mile and a half I should think. I got into the strangest places, among the wildest Neapolitans – kitchens, washing-places, archways, stables, vineyards – was baited by dogs, answered in profoundly unintelligible Neapolitan, from behind lonely locked doors, in cracked female voices, quaking with fear; could hear of no such Englishman or any Englishman. By-and-by I came upon a Polenta-shop in the clouds, where an old Frenchman, with an umbrella like a faded tropical leaf (it had not rained for six weeks) was staring at nothing at all, with a snuff-box in his hand. To him I appealed concerning the Signor Larthoor. 'Sir', said he, with the sweetest politeness, 'can you speak French?' 'Sir', said I, 'a little.' 'Sir', said he, 'I presume the Signor Loothere' – you will observe that he changed the name according to the custom of his country – 'is an Englishman.' I admitted that he was the victim of circumstances and had that misfortune. 'Sir', said he, 'one word more. *Has* he a servant with a wooden leg?' 'Great Heaven, sir', said I, 'how do I know! I should think not, but it is possible.' 'It is always', said the Frenchman, 'possible. Almost all the things of the world are always possible.' 'Sir', said I – you may imagine my condition and dismal sense of my own absurdity, by this time – 'that is true.' He then took an immense pinch of snuff, wiped the dust off his umbrella, led me to an arch commanding a wonderful view of the bay of Naples, and pointed deep into the earth from which I had mounted. 'Below there, near the lamp, one finds an Englishman, with a servant with a wooden leg. It is always possible that he is the Signor Loothere.' I had been asked at six, and it was now getting on for seven. I went down again in a state of perspiration and misery not to be described, and without the faintest hope of finding the place. But as I was going down to the lamp, I saw the strangest staircase up a dark corner, with a man in a white waistcoat (evidently hired) standing on the top of it, fuming. I dashed in at a venture, found it was the place, made the most of the whole story, and was indescribably popular. The best of it was, that as nobody ever did find the place, he had put a servant at the bottom of the Salita, to 'wait for an English gentleman'. The servant (as he presently pleaded), deceived by the moustache, had allowed the English gentleman to pass unchallenged.

Hommage à l'illustre écrivain d'Angleterre

As time went on and he returned again and again to Paris, Dickens was to discover that the standing of writers there was very different from the humble one accorded to them in London. In a letter to Forster, in January 1856, he described a magnificent banquet given in his honour by Monsieur Girardin who had made his fortune in publishing.

THE BANQUET

No man unacquainted with my determination never to embellish or fancify such accounts, could believe in the description I shall let off when we meet of dining at Emile Girardin's – of the three gorgeous drawing rooms with ten thousand wax candles in golden sconces, terminating in a dining-room of unprecedented magnificence with two enormous transparent plate-glass doors in it, looking (across an ante-chamber full of clean plates) straight into the kitchen, with the cooks in their white paper caps dishing the dinner. From his seat in the midst of the table, the host (like a Giant in a Fairy story) beholds the kitchen, and the snow-white tables, and the profound order and silence there prevailing. Forth from the plate-glass doors issues the Banquet – the most wonderful feast ever tasted by mortal: at the present price of Truffles, that article alone costing (for eight people) at least five pounds. On the table are ground glass jugs of peculiar construction, laden with the finest growth of Champagne and the coolest ice. With the third course is issued Port Wine (previously unheard of in a good state on this continent), which would fetch two guineas a bottle at any sale. The dinner done, Oriental flowers in vases of golden cobweb are placed upon the board. With the ice is issued Brandy, buried for 100 years. To that succeeds Coffee, brought by the brother of one of the convives from the remotest East, in exchange for an equal quantity of Californian gold dust. The company being returned to the drawing-room – tables roll in by unseen agency, laden with Cigarettes from the Hareem of the Sultan, and with cool drinks in which the flavour of the Lemon arrived yesterday from Algeria, struggles voluptuously with the delicate Orange arrived this morning from Lisbon. That period past, and the guests reposing on Divans worked with many-coloured blossoms, big table rolls in, heavy with massive furniture of silver, and breathing incense in the form of a little present of Tea direct from China – table and all, I believe; but cannot swear to it, and am resolved to be prosaic. All this time the host perpetually repeats 'Ce petit dîner-ci n'est que pour faire la connaissance de Monsieur Dickens; il ne compte pas; ce n'est rien'. And even now I have forgotten to set down half of it – in particular the item of a far larger plum pudding than ever was seen in England at Christmas time, served with a celestial sauce in colour like the orange blossom, and in substance like the blossom powdered and bathed in dew, and called in the carte (carte in a gold frame like a little fish-slice to be handed about) 'Hommage à l'illustre écrivain d'Angleterre'. That illustrious man staggered out at the last drawing-room door, speechless with wonder, finally; and even at that moment his host, holding to his lips a chalice set with precious stones and containing nectar distilled from the air that blew over the fields of beans in bloom for fifteen summers, remarked 'Le dîner que nous avons eu, mon cher, n'est rien – il ne compte pas – il a été tout-à-fait en famille – il faur dîner (en vérité, dîner) bientôt. Au plaisir! Au revoir! Au dîner!'

Dickens renewed his acquaintance with famous literary figures and was introduced to others, including George Sand, whom he was astonished to find 'had nothing of the blue stocking about her, except a little final way of settling all your opinions with hers'. But, in appearance, he thought she was just the kind of woman 'who might have been the Queen's monthly nurse'. To Forster he described his impressions of Lamartine.

He continued to be precisely as we knew him, both in appearance and manner; highly prepossessing, and with a sort of calm passion about him, very taking indeed . . . I found him frank and unaffected and full of curious knowledge of the French common people. He informed the company at dinner that he had rarely met a foreigner who spoke French so easily as your inimitable correspondent, whereat your correspondent blushed modestly, and almost immediately afterwards so nearly choked himself with the bone of a fowl (which is still in his throat) that he sat in torture for ten minutes with a strong apprehension that he was going to make the good Pichot famous by dying like the little Hunchback at his table.

Dickens grew more and more fluent in speaking and writing French, though he did not fall in love with it as he had done with Italian. To his regret he never learned German. But the translations of his books into that language had continued steadily ever since 1838 and, in 1841, he had begun his long connexion with Baron Tauchnitz. Soon they had made a friendly agreement by which Dickens allowed him to print his novels from his own marked proof copies and to publish them in his famous paperback Tauchnitz edition. Baron Tauchnitz also advised him in the preparation, in 1855, of an agreement for a translation into French of all his novels and stories.

In that year the daily paper, Moniteur, *was publishing* Chuzzlewit, *and Dickens found that directly he went into any shop and produced his card he was greeted with a flood of excited questions or comments about his book. A few years later the translations were being displayed on every bookstall.*

All this time, his fame not only as a writer but also as reader of his own books to larger and larger audiences was steadily growing. In January 1863 he gave a reading in the British Embassy in Paris to an audience which included many who did not know a word of English. Nevertheless they seemed to understand and appreciate every word and gesture, and he himself was stimulated as never before. A second reading was called for a few days later. 'Blazes of Triumph' *he wrote ecstatically.*

Return via Staplehurst

In spite of all his success, however, Dickens had been growing more and more unhappy in his married life and, in 1858, he and Catherine had separated. From then on he began to spend more and more time in France, sometimes taking with him the young actress Ellen Ternan, with whom he had fallen desperately in love. On the afternoon of 9 June 1865 they were returning together when the boat-train in which they were travelling to London was derailed at Staplehurst in Kent. It was a frightful accident, but, by a miracle, Dickens and Ellen happened to be in the only carriage that did not topple over the steep embankment. Except for the shock, Dickens was unhurt, and four days later he wrote a graphic account to his friend Mitton.

THE ACCIDENT

I was in the only carriage that did not go over into the stream. It was caught upon the turn by some of the ruin of the bridge, and hung suspended and balanced in an apparently impossible manner. Two ladies were my fellow-passengers, an old one and a young one. This is exactly what passed. You may judge from it the precise length of the suspense; suddenly we were off the rail, and beating the ground as the car of a half-emptied balloon might. The old lady cried out, 'My God!' and the young one screamed. I caught hold of them both (the old lady sat opposite and the young one on my left) and said: 'We can't help ourselves, but we can be quiet and composed. Pray don't cry out.' The old lady immediately answered; 'Thank you. Rely upon me. Upon my soul I will be quiet.' We were then all tilted down together in a corner of the carriage, and stopped. I said to them thereupon: 'You may be sure nothing worse can happen. Our

Dickens relieving the sufferers of the first fatal railway accident near Staplehurst, 9 June 1865

danger *must* be over. Will you remain here without stirring, while I get out of the window?' They both answered quite collectedly, 'Yes', and I got out without the least notion what had happened. Fortunately I got out with great caution and stood upon the step. Looking down I saw the bridge gone, and nothing below me but the line of rail. Some people in the two other compartments were madly trying to plunge out at window [*sic*], and had no idea that there was an open swampy field fifteen feet below them, and nothing else! The two guards (one with his face cut) were running up and down on the down side of the bridge (which was not torn up) quite wildly. I called out to them, 'Look at me. Do stop an instant and look at me, and tell me whether you don't know me.' One of them answered; 'We know you very well, Mr Dickens'. 'Then', I said, 'my good fellow, for God's sake give me your key, and send one of your labourers here, and I'll empty this carriage'. We did it quite safely, by means of a plank or two, and when it was done I saw all the rest of the train, except the two baggage vans, down in the stream. I got into the carriage again for my brandy flask, took off my travelling hat for a basin, climbed down the brick-work, and filled my hat with water.

Suddenly I came upon a staggering man covered with blood (I think he must have been flung clean out of his carriage), with such a frightful cut across the skull that I couldn't bear to look at him. I poured some water over his face and gave him some to drink, then gave him some brandy, and laid him down on the grass, and he said, 'I am gone', and died afterwards. Then I stumbled over a lady lying on her back against a little pollard-tree, with the blood streaming over her face (which was lead colour) in a number of distinct little streams from the head. I asked her if she could swallow a little brandy and she just nodded, and I gave her some and left her for somebody else. The next time I passed her she was dead. Then a man, examined at the inquest yesterday, (who evidently had not the least remembrance of what really passed), came running up to me and implored me to help him find his wife, who was afterwards found dead. No imagination can conceive the ruin of the carriages, or the extraordinary weights under which people were lying, or the complications into which they were twisted up among iron and wood, and mud and water.

I don't want to be examined at the inquest, and I don't want to write about it. I could do no good either way, and I could only seem to speak about myself, which, of course, I would rather not do. I am keeping very quiet here. I have a – I don't know what to call it – constitutional (I suppose) presence of mind, and was not in the least fluttered at the time. I instantly remembered that I had the MS of a number with me, and clambered back into the carriage for it. But in writing these scanty words of recollection I feel the shake and am obliged to stop.

As many grateful letters afterwards testified, Dickens' own account of what he did on this ghastly occasion gives only the minimal truth, but the picture of the compassionate fellow-traveller with his brandy flask and his hatful of river water will never be forgotten. He behaved throughout the crisis with characteristic coolness and initiative, and only when he had done all he could for the injured and dying did he climb back for the second time into the precariously-balanced carriage to retrieve the latest instalment of Our Mutual Friend. *But as, clasping his precious dishevelled manuscript, he edged himself once again out of the dangerous window he knew that death had touched him on the shoulder. When his book was published, he wrote in a Postscript: 'I can never be much nearer to parting with my readers forever than I was then'.*

In spite of all his pleasure in the countrified ways of life which he now enjoyed at Gadshill, the last five years of Dickens' life are predominantly a distressful record of hectic living – of stupendous public readings and a wildly-mad second tour of America. Successful, yes, but far beyond his physical powers. Staplehurst had had such a shattering effect upon his whole constitution that it is a wonder he ever had the nerve to cross the Channel again, for it had been the vagaries of his old enemy the Channel-tide, allied to human idiocy in the small matter of misreading the railway time-table, that had caused the accident.

At home in the Swiss chalet

Dickens did, however, go to France again as soon as in September of the same year, and this was by no means his last visit. Now too, in his own garden at Gadshill, he had a constant reminder not only of his French friend, the actor Charles Fechter, but also of the happy days he had spent in Switzerland. This was nothing less than a Swiss chalet which (in ninety-five separate pieces!) Fechter had sent him and which, with suitable assistance, Dickens had set up in his orchard garden across the road.

In this delightful little wooden house among the tree-tops alive with singing birds whose every movement was reflected in the mirrors all round him, Dickens spent many happy and rewarding hours. And perhaps it was due to those long quiet sessions that, alternating with scenes of dramatic intensity for which his last novel, Edwin Drood, *is so unforgettable, many passages give the feeling that here, in his deeper maturity, is still the essential Dickens of* Pictures from Italy. *It was on* Edwin Drood *that he was working in his chalet for most of 8 June 1870. After returning to his house in the evening, he suffered a severe stroke from which he never recovered consciousness. He died the next day. He was only fifty-eight.*

Everything he wrote during those last hours has a special poignancy, but nothing is so treasured for its own sake as one passage in Edwin Drood *which is radiant with his love of natural life and his Christian belief in the supernatural.*

Perhaps for him mere 'time' already no longer counted, and what had happened twenty-five years ago had imperceptibly merged into his present. However that may have been, it is clear that in writing of his experience in the precincts of his own Rochester cathedral, he must have been remembering also what he had seen to delight him in 'the retired Piazza' of Parma one day in November 1844.

. . . ancient buildings of a sombre brown, embellished with innumerable grotesque monsters and dreamy-looking creatures carved in marble and red stone – are clustered in a noble and magnificent repose. Their silent presence was invaded, when I saw them, by the twittering of the many birds that were flying in and out of the crevices in the stones and little nooks in the architecture where thay had made their nests. They were busy, rising from the cold shade of Temples made with hands, into the sunny air of Heaven.

And then, the passage from Edwin Drood.

Changes of glorious light from moving boughs, songs of birds, scents from gardens, woods and fields, – or rather from the one great garden of the cultivated island – penetrate into the Cathedral, subdue its earthy odour, and preach the Resurrection and the Life. The cold stone tombs of centuries old grow warm; and flecks of brightness dart into the sternest marble corners of the building, fluttering there like wings.

Set in 'Monotype' Bell 11 point leaded 1 point.
Printed by W & J Mackay Limited, Chatham,
text by letterpress and illustrations by litho,
on Publishers' Reserve paper.
Bound in buckram cloth by
W & J Mackay Limited.

LONDON
Gadshill
Dover
Calais
Boulogne
BELGIUM
PARIS
FRANCE
SWITZE
Lausanne
Geneva
Marseilles
SPAIN